W9-AMB-070

PERSPECTIVES--

FROM THE
CORNFIELD
TO THE
CLUBHOUSE

GENE HENSLEY

WITH ILLUSTRATIONS BY

GEORGIA LEE FARR

PERSPECTIVES...

FROM THE CORNFIELD TO THE CLUBHOUSE

By

GENE HENSLEY

© 2005 GENE HENSLEY
All Rights Reserved.

No part of this book may be reproduced, stored in a retrieval system, or transmitted by any means without the written permission of the author.

First published by AuthorHouse 12/20/04

ISBN: 1-4208-0299-2 (sc)

Library of Congress Control Number: 2004098797

Printed in the United States of America
Bloomington, Indiana

This book is printed on acid-free paper.

authorHOUSE

1663 LIBERTY DRIVE
BLOOMINGTON, INDIANA 47403
(800) 839-8640
www.authorhouse.com

ABOUT PERSPECTIVES....

Each of us is a product of our birth, background and the bountiful legacy of life shaping events - good or bad - which make us who we are. Beyond genetic considerations, we are contained in our personal development and knowledge by the scope of these unique life experiences.

This, in turn, dictates how we look at things and gives us our own individual perspectives on life.

These are some of mine. As they are now. They will differ from yours simply because they are mine. But, although we started from different places and sometimes stumbled in our own separate footsteps to get us to where we are, maybe we really aren't all that far apart.

The tracks that each of us leave in life are marked by the changes each new perspective brings as it enters an open mind. We never know where it may lead us; but it can remind us of where we have been. That, in itself, may be helpful as we continue along our individual paths through this amazing evolution called life.

I acknowledge, with gratitude, the delightful set of original pen and ink illustrations, contributed as a "work for hire" by Georgia Lee Farr, whose work is reflected in the smaller versions used in the narratives. The color for the inserts was added by Patricia Worley. Both Georgia Lee and Patti are from Jeffersonville, Indiana.

I hope you enjoy the book.

Gene Hensley, Jeffersonville, Indiana
Original Copyright: May 1, 1986
Revised: June 12, 2003

PERSPECTIVES

FROM THE CORNFIELD TO THE CLUBHOUSE

Table of Contents

ON PERSPECTIVES

Who would have thought I would have needed the eyes of a professionally acclaimed photographer to see where I grew up?

Those constantly curious, scenery-sensitive, eyes belonged to my brother-in-law, Ronald Justice, who, with his wife, Ruth, had relocated to Welch, West Virginia from their hometown of Pikeville, Kentucky. I had begun my business career in Welch, some twenty miles from my own hometown, and it was there that I met my future wife, Elizabeth, while she was on a brief visit with her sister. Shortly thereafter, I was transferred by my company to, of all places, Pikeville, Kentucky. Life takes strange turns sometimes. Although we now lived several high mountains and a hard three-hour drive apart, Ron and I had virtually exchanged hometowns.

In time - and with my marriage to Elizabeth - relocations and deaths among the members of my immediate family left Ron and Ruth as our only close relatives remaining in West Virginia. Visiting with them occasionally gave me a chance, of sorts, to go back home.

Home, for me, was a hillside farm that seemed to grow rocks better than anything else; and, my memories of childhood always are somewhat clouded by the rigors of life in those mountains. A young boy growing up there had to work hard to help the family survive.

Summers were hot, winters were hard and there was always more to do than you could ever get done. There were trees to cut down and split up for firewood; water to carry from the spring for drinking, washing and livestock; weeds to pull for the hogs in summer and fodder to carry to the horses in winter.

And, inevitably, year after year, there was field after rocky field of corn to hoe in the summertime.

That's what I remember most, hoeing corn. It never ended from spring until fall. As the cornstalks grew and tasseled, the leaves would cut the skin and pollen would soak into the cuts to itch you like crazy, helped along by the running sweat that literally poured out of your body on those hot summer days. That brought even more irritation in the form of those small, pesky sweat bees that followed you all day long, usually landing and crawling around on your upper back or arms, provoking you until you slapped at them, which made you cut yourself on another leaf of the corn stalk, which caused the stalk to shake, which caused more pollen to fall.

In addition to that, you could usually count on an occasional snake or yellow jacket to stop by the row you were hoeing just to see if you had reached your misery quotient yet.

For a boy growing up in those cornfields, the mountains were a barrier. Some people lived out their entire lives there and had never been to Beckley, less than fifty miles away. The Sears Roebuck catalog was our department store and the short order grills at a local tavern and cabstand were what passed for our restaurants. If the town's hotel had a dining facility, I never saw it.

When you grew up, unless you could go to college and become a schoolteacher, your career choices were the mines, timbering or the military service. Shortly after I finished high school, I joined the army. Even with a war going on, I joined anyway. It was better than what I had to look forward to.

That's why, when Elizabeth and I were visiting Ron and Ruth a few years later, a comment he made had such a personal impact.

Ron and I were playing golf at his home club and there in the middle of a fairway, maybe in the middle of a swing, he suddenly stopped and looked around with sincere appreciation and wonder through those restless, searching, photographer's eyes.

"Aren't those mountains beautiful!'" he said.

I suppose that in his moment of inspired thought, he had forgotten that I was not just a casual visitor to his adopted state. But something besides a mental camera shutter must have clicked.

Since then I have been to other golf courses carved out of those mountains and, more recently, to one near my old hometown. It had an attractively appointed clubhouse; and, as I had lunch at a table by the window, the view was truly magnificent.

The neatly groomed fairways followed the gently rolling contours of a mountain meadow across a spring-fed brook to the edge of the forest. Rhododendron and other flowering plants and trees provided a colorful edging within a majestic framework of cool, inviting mountains. It was as pretty as a picture.

Still I couldn't help but wonder if, on the other side of the mountain, some young boy wasn't out there in the sun taking up the vigil against the rocks, the weeds, the snakes, and the sweat bees as he daydreamed about crossing those mountains to a better life.

You have plenty of time to do that hoeing corn.

In reflection, though, I have to admit that personal perspectives can change. Those mountains are, indeed, beautiful.

It's just that an awful lot depends on whether you are looking at them from the clubhouse or the cornfield.

ON MARRIAGE

I believe in marriage. But I also know that all marriages are not destined to last. Some of the ones that do probably shouldn't.

There are plenty of good reasons why a couple should call it quits when the odds against a long, happy marriage start stacking up. On the other hand, there are plenty of bad reasons why marriages fail.

The worst of these, in my opinion, is the one a friend of mine gave me one time on the occasion of his divorce.

"I just outgrew her," he said.

The arrogance of that statement takes me back to a similar comment, in the form of well-intentioned advice, which I received from my first employer.

He knew I was thinking about getting married and he thought I had a promising future with the company. His advice to me, reflecting perhaps his own frustrations with an on-again, off-again domestic situation, was "Son, marry a school teacher. She'll help you grow." Perhaps his own wife was lacking in the qualities he now found important as hostess or helpmate to his new self-image.

Quite honestly, it was not the boardroom I was thinking about when Elizabeth and I got married. I was twenty-two and she was two years younger, neither of us had gone to college and both of us were from rural backgrounds.

In fact, I felt rather proud of myself for having landed a girl as pretty and personable as Elizabeth. Besides that, there just weren't that many school teachers, attractive or otherwise, chasing me around.

Over the years, though, I have changed as all of us do. But when I did go to college, earning two degrees before I was through, it was Elizabeth who kept up the house, cut the grass, cared for the kids and spent endless hours with the little league, boy scouts, girl scouts, P.T.A. and all those other child-raising functions that lay claim to a responsible parent's time.

I worked all day, went to school at night and studied on weekends. She thought I was working too hard and tried to make it easy on me.

There were times, I know, when Elizabeth had some concern as she watched me grow in responsibility, social skills and education. She was afraid that she

3

would be left behind or would not fit into my new future. I always reassured her that any progress I made in life was her progress too.

Even as she continued to be mother and father to the children; housekeeper and maintenance person for our home; and, a producer of extra income as a safety net for the family when things became tight, she still had doubts. But she was in it for better or for worse with a child-like trust that something intangible, called love, would see us through.

Those anxious moments are long behind us now. The kids grew up just fine and my very satisfying career ended long ago. During it all, I tried to share everything I did with her. And when I presented her to my new friends or acquaintances, I did so with the same pride I still feel today. She remains, as she did those many years ago, a beautiful woman and, more important, a very beautiful person.

One of the reasons, I believe, is that I never looked for faults in Elizabeth and she never looked for any in me. We always stood as a common front against all the obstacles that ever came our way. Even where we didn't have mutual interest, we always had mutual respect.

Through it all, when the intellects got a little too intellectual; the sophisticates too sophisticated; or, the snobs a little too snobbish; if it was that way for her, it was that way for me.

That's why, I guess, of all the reasons for divorce I've ever heard, "I outgrew her," has to be the most arrogant of all to me.

During my modest trek through life, I have eagerly accepted and vainly displayed most of the educational and professional credentials, as well as the various civic and scholastic honors and awards, which I have earned.

Prominently placed, from the very beginning, among those prized documents and plaques is a large, framed colored photograph of Elizabeth. It was taken when she was nineteen, shortly before we were married. Without her love, devotion and support, the wall would be blank. She always has been, and will always be, an integral part of anything - and everything - that we, together, have accomplished in life.

How do you ever outgrow that?

ON HUMILITY

Back when I was in high school, during the early fifties, there was this short-lived thing called the look of love.

Emulating the Hollywood heartthrobs of the day, supposedly any boy could cast his sexiest gaze at the girl of his choice, holding her attention until -

almost hypnotically - she was his. I had mirror-perfected mine and was ready for a trial run.

The ideal time came during a study period in our biology class. Always being a person who hedged his risks, I finally decided to go with someone other than a beauty queen; but, being reasonably confident at that point, I surely didn't want to end up with the ugliest girl in the room following me around the schoolhouse for the rest of the afternoon.

I picked out Helen, two rows away, who fell somewhere in between.

At first, I thought it was working.

My Humphrey Bogart brooding eyes, Montgomery Clift vulnerability and Clark Gable knowing smile combined the best of irresistible images I was sure, so I focused them upon her as I leaned casually forward on my desk.

Her eyes darted toward me, then back to her papers, then back to me again.

I had gotten her attention.

After giving her my best shot for a minute or so, I could tell she was losing her self-control. It was that look of mounting passion on her face.

And then, soon thereafter, she gave in, breaking the silence of the study period with some of the most memorable words of my life: "What's the matter with you, boy? I ain't got your meat skin!"

I was crushed.

Helen had just equated my sexiest look to the plea of a starving hound dog begging for a scrap of food - and disrupted the whole class in the process. Then, the pain of her explanation to the teacher!

That was the first real humility builder I remember, and the one I lean on the most when I feel myself getting just a little too cocky from time to time. The humor I later found in that incident always reminds me what can happen when a person takes himself too seriously.

That was years ago and there has never been a shortage of people to build upon the foundation Helen laid for me that day. Drill sergeants, music publishers, college math teachers, karate kids with big black belts and a myriad of others have been more than generous in their application of new layers.

Even my close friend and brother-in-law, Ron Justice, gave me a harmonica for Christmas one year. He said it really was a gift for the whole family since he knew I couldn't play the harmonica and sing at the same time.

The most recent layer, although milder than most, came from no less an icon of worldwide commerce than the Daimler Chrysler Corporation. I had purchased a new Jeep Grand Cherokee Limited for my wife in celebration of her sixty-fifth birthday. It was titled in both names but, since it was her car, her name came first. The dealer told us we would be receiving a survey from corporate headquarters to gain our input on the level of service we had experienced from their sales staff. A few weeks later the survey arrived - addressed to "Mr. and Mrs. Elizabeth Hensley".

I now realize, for me at least, that the process of developing humility has been much like the forming of a coral reef, except that the cutting edge is directed more inward than out. Yet, through it all, when I have recognized that a new layer was being applied, I could always face it with full knowledge that I had survived much worse before.

I've even had the pleasure of seeing a little humility applied to others. My favorite instance happened during the "Happy Dollar" segment of our Rotary Club program where a member could pay a dollar - accumulated for our charitable efforts - to make an announcement about something pleasant that had just happened to him or her, a family member or someone else in the community the rest of us would know. On this occasion one of our more pompous members paid his dollar and announced, with a little too much pride and swagger, his recent promotion to Captain in the naval reserves. He then went to great lengths to educate us on the fact that a Captain in the Navy was the equivalent of a full bird Colonel in the Army, one step below Brigadier General, and that it entitled the holder of that prestigious rank to wear scrambled eggs on his hat and so on. When he had finally finished with his lengthy and ingratiating tribute to himself, a younger member paid his Happy Dollar and made his own quick, pointed announcement: "I'm a First Lieutenant in the Army Reserves. When I get promoted again, I will be a real Captain."

So it goes with most of us as we pass through life. But Helen, the classmate from that old "look of love" experiment, gave me one last disappointment a few years ago.

I had told Elizabeth this story and she appreciated it so much, that I was delighted to see Helen among those attending my twenty-five year high school reunion. I introduced her to Elizabeth and recalled the incident and its importance to me over time. Helen, gracious lady that she's become, confessed she didn't remember the incident at all.

Maybe that's the best way to learn humility, where the source quickly forgets and the object long remembers.

But somehow it seems a little sad that a moment so important in my life could have been so inconsequential in hers.

On the other hand, perhaps the debt one owes to those who helped develop his or her humility is better repaid to others through the courtesy and understanding that true humility breeds.

In the case of that newly commissioned Navy Captain, maybe not.

Anyway, Helen, thanks.

ON POVERTY

I grew up in poverty. We all did. Everybody who lived on our creek was poor. About a mile away, at the mouth of the creek, there was a small grocery store. About four miles in the other direction at the head of the creek was virgin wilderness, complete with a working beaver dam. Everyone who lived in between scratched out a living the best way they could.

It wasn't that we were ever homeless or starving: we raised our own food; owned our own small house; carried our water from a spring; cut our own firewood; and, provided our own entertainment. But, there was no telephone, no electricity and no running water until I was in my teens.

Somewhere around that grocery store, they had all those things but that also was the dividing line in the school district. The kids with running water and inside johns went to school in town; we went to school in the country. No running water at home, no running water at school; no big deal.

We only had twenty-five kids or so in our little one room school, grade primer through eight. Those who lived close enough went home for lunch. My brother, cousins and I took ours.

Usually lunch was a bacon and biscuit sandwich that fast food restaurants have popularized in recent years. Back then, it meant you couldn't afford store bought bread and luncheon meat. That didn't make any difference in grade school. High school was another story. A greasy, overused paper lunch bag is hard to hide.

Until high school all the people I knew worked hard for what little money they had. My father and uncle ran a small sawmill and timbering operation. In summer, my younger brother and I earned meager amounts of spending money by tying cap wedges at the mill for two and one-half cents a bundle or hoeing corn for people for a quarter an hour.

One summer I also sold packets of seeds and Cloverine salve for the prizes offered by the companies. They always looked exotic and very tempting in the recruiting advertisements: an airplane cockpit, watches - things kids like us only dreamed of. The cockpit turned out to be nothing but a cheap cardboard facsimile and the Ingraham pocket watch sold for about a dollar in the Sears Roebuck catalog.

With money so scarce, we mostly traded things. My experience began with a real butt burner. When I was nine or ten, I traded a pedal car, which was rusty but still in good condition, for about two hundred marbles. One wheel off the car would have been worth more than those marbles. But everyone starts somewhere, and I got better at it.

When my older brothers came home from time to time they would give me something like a pocketknife or a broken watch to see what I could do with it. Through a series of trades, a beautifully encased but functionally useless watch turned into a seventeen-jewel Elgin watch and fifteen dollars. My brothers got a kick out of things like that.

While I didn't realize it at the time, trading things taught me a lot about life. The value of a possession changes, or can be made to change, in the hands of its owner. Once a person owns something and gets used to having it around, the less important it becomes. If you kept your eye out and maneuvered the right trades, you could end up with some comparatively nice things. At various times I had my hands on many items that others considered of value; a bicycle, a .22 rifle, a pair of western style leather fringed gloves, a Stetson hat. Stetsons were popular with the loggers who worked for my dad. They would trade almost anything for a good one.

Getting your hands on real money was something else. One time I found ten dollars laying beside the road. That was a small fortune to me; forty hours of hoeing corn or four hundred bundles of cap wedges.

My first thought was to tell the local grocery store owner, in case he had heard who lost it. I knew it had to be somebody who needed it because that's all we had living around there. Fortunately I was still a quarter of a mile away from the store and, by the time I got there, the struggle with my conscience had passed. Relying on my good Baptist upbringing, I just put the money in my pocket and kept my mouth shut. I figured God must have wanted me to have it. If He didn't, why did He show me where it was?

When I started to high school, I began to sense a class distinction. I now realize that many of the kids I thought were "rich" were only a notch above poverty themselves. Ours was principally a coal mining community; and, mining companies, at that time, were notorious for keeping their employees captive, as consumers and debtors, to their rental housing, company stores and other goods and services they provided. But perception is reality; I only knew what I saw. Those kids lived in nicer houses, wore better clothes, most received small allowances and some had access to a family car. I had none of those things and it affected my full assimilation into that new culture. Within such personal conflicts of poverty and pride there are, undoubtedly, many missed opportunities for stronger friendships and better memories.

Except for writing a few book reports for a quarter apiece, I had little access to spending money during the school year. Morning and evening chores

8

prevented my participation in extra-curricular activities and a lack of transportation dictated my adherence to a strict school bus schedule.

My primary clothing outfit, during my senior year, was an ill-fitting sport coat, sport shirt, slacks and shoes that my brother, Ralph, gave me when he re-enlisted in the military service. I wore out those clothes, down to cardboard in the soles of the shoes, by wearing them practically every day. The coat and shirt are commemorated in our Year Book staff picture. The faculty advisor, a woman I greatly admired, personally encouraged me to participate. I assumed it was because she thought I could contribute and appreciated my good grades. I always had been proud of that rare special attention I had received from a favored teacher and mentioned it to a classmate some years later. She told me that I, undoubtedly, was mistaken. The Year Book project was open to any class member, regardless of other considerations. There are people in life who blow you an occasional bubble; there are others whose job it is to burst them. Ah, yes, even very small bubbles.

So, I went through high school as invisible as possible, spending my junior year in California and reducing my senior year, for all practical purposes, to a single semester.

For those first two years, I was always glad to see summer come - not because of the coursework, but to get back into a more comfortable world. Had I seen any reasonable options, I may have dropped out of school like so many others did when they reached sixteen. However, my desire to receive that high school diploma, and maybe go on to college, proved to be stronger than any such negative thoughts.

During the final semester of my senior year, I tested out of all but one class. The teacher said his own daughter wasn't smart enough to test out of his class and so he was sure I couldn't. He may have been right; we will never know.

That left me with time for a job, which I finally found in a poolroom. I worked until almost midnight every night, except Sunday, for pocket change. But I did learn to shoot pool and if I count my winnings while I was in the Army, I did okay. That was because I always tried to follow the advice of Charlie Stepp, the owner of that poolroom: Never gamble with someone you can't beat.

It was in the Army, the following year, that I became acquainted with people who literally changed my life. I was assigned to a division of N.A.T.O. that was considered a prime duty station. Some of the draftees arriving there could trace their assignment to family influence or political favor. A friend of mine from basic training and I, both having failed the final interview process for Officers Candidate School, tested for it and were the only successful applicants from the entire Fourth Army.

We were sent to the Allied Land Forces Central Europe command at Fontainebleau, France. There, all evidence of economic or social differences suddenly disappeared. In that environment, we all wore the same clothes, ate the same food, slept in the same barracks, participated in the same activities, and had similar jobs.

Almost everyone I came to know there were genuinely nice, intelligent and highly motivated people. One of them hired another soldier to take my turn as Charge-of-Quarters on my last Christmas Eve in France. In their minds, Pete and Peggy Koukos were not doing anything special; they just wanted some of their friends to join them for dinner that evening and didn't want me to be left out. But such duty changes also require command clearance and the resolution of other issues. Few people would have gone to the trouble.

It was serving with such people that gave me my first real sense of what it takes to be successful in life. I already had some level of ambition and determination; what I was learning was character and compassion.

In my childhood, as with all poor people, there were hardships, humiliations and embarrassments. I have tried to spare my own children these. Sometimes we, who do this, overcompensate and end up with spoiled kids. I hope I haven't done that. But I can say that two of my strongest ambitions from growing up poor have been achieved.

One was to own a car with a heater. This was born, nurtured and reinforced too many times to remember on those bitter cold nights walking the five miles home from the poolroom. Sometimes I would hitch a ride and when someone stopped and I climbed inside, the car would be as warm as a mother's love. I can still feel the chill wearing off at times.

The other goal was not so lofty.

I promised myself if I could ever afford it, I would buy a full five-pound can of spiced luncheon meat - the kind I remembered with mouth watering envy from my early days in high school. When I finally did, I think I must have picked up a bad can. The meat was grainy and didn't taste very good at all. I ended up throwing most of it away.

I was afraid it might be that way when I bought it. But when you grow up poor, you remember.

A promise is a promise.

ON ELVIS

Every true Elvis Presley fan can tell you everything about the man: when and where he was born; how many movies he made; how many gold records he had; and, everything else you did or didn't want to know. I reluctantly admit that I'm an admirer myself and consider him to be the best raw talent of my lifetime. But there's the rub. You see, Elvis and I were born the same year, in 1935. He was born in January; I was born in June.

The problem is that there is only so much good looks and talent to go around; and, I believe to this day that whoever was passing it out when he was born got carried away and he got more than he should have. By the time June rolled around, there wasn't much left and they started skimping on everything. So here I am, late in life, banging on a guitar I can't play, writing songs I can't sell and looking like anything but a handsome, leading man; all because some grand dispenser of genetic tidbits went to sleep at the switch in January and I wasn't born until June. There's absolutely no question in my mind that this master error has been the reason that everything I have tried to accomplish in life has been marred by mediocrity and broken bones.

"We're running low on talent," they must have said. "Just give him a little so he'll have the taste of it but, remember, we've got over half the year left to go."

That surely must have happened with my ration of looks, talent, and calcium. Except I always thought they might have let up a little on some things like humility, sensitivity, charm and things like that. I say this because I once knew a man who was born later on that year and he didn't have any of these. I guess they had used them all up by November. That's the only thing I figure could have happened.

Anyway, I know that Elvis made good use of all the talent and resources he was given, and I'm not complaining. Besides, it could have been a lot worse for all of us born later that year.

In my own case, I could have been born on December 31. If you recall, 1935 was right in the middle of the Great Depression and my family wouldn't have even needed the break on income taxes. But there I'd be anyway, one day away from a brand new pool of talent going out in 1936, being born late at night on December 31, 1935. I can only imagine what a combination of hair, nose, chin, ears and other bits and pieces would have been left by then. They probably would have just thrown it all together, whatever they had left, and that would have been me.

Still, I don't hold any animosity. In fact, I have fond memories of Elvis, like most people of my age, and feel a special kinship through sharing that common year of birth. But, don't you agree that this kind of thing shouldn't happen?

Maybe when Congress gets through with all those trivial things like budget deficits, nuclear war and social security, they can get busy on the real issue; the one that could have prevented all this: equal rights. The Constitution acknowledges that all men are created equal but, frankly, I always thought Elvis was created way more equal than me. The Bill of Rights is supposed to protect against travesties like that. Just because somebody is born in January and some geneticrat goes to sleep at the switch...

I just think it's time we did something about this kind of stupid mistake.

ON PETS

Dogs are dogs. Every farm boy knows that. They are working animals that stake out their territorial limits and protect it against all comers, man or beast.

We had two dogs when I was growing up, Cap and Sarge. They were a beautiful mixed breed of German shepherd and hound and big enough to drape their feet over my shoulders even after I reached my full height of six feet. And they could be as mean as they were big and beautiful. Except to us. My brother and I got them when they were pups and we all grew up together.

Aside from their companionship, I always felt safe with the dogs around. Even on those long walks back from town in the dead of night after seeing

a Frankenstein or a Wolf Man movie, when the moonlight cast strange images through the trees and the rippling of the creek sounded just like footsteps, all I had to do was make it to our fence line. When I got within range, I could outrun whatever was after me in those woods. Then I could rest. Cap and Sarge would be waiting by the gate.

In their later years, Sarge developed a problem with his feet and we gave him to a veterinarian who said he would take care of him. Cap died while I was in military service overseas. The letter my dad wrote me about that must have been as hard for him to write as it was for me to read. I knew the exact spot where he said he buried Cap. It was under one of our favorite shade trees on the edge of the upper cornfield, where Cap would come to rest with me between hoeing rows of corn.

When my children were still very young, I wanted them to have a dog. As soon as we built a fence, without telling anyone, I went to a pet store to pick one out. He picked me out instead.

As I walked by the cages, a little black cocker barely six weeks old greeted me with an enthusiasm that stopped me in my tracks. He knew I had come for him and, at that moment, I did too.

My son named him Bullet because of the way he darted from hand to hand that day, meeting each member of his new family with the same enthusiasm he showed at the pet shop. And through the years, except for being constrained to the back yard of a subdivision, he did all the things that Cap had done as companion, protector and friend.

That back yard became his personal territory and he guarded it with a passion. When he barred his white teeth against a mane of black bristling hair he could send chills through anybody.

He stayed outside, only coming in the family room at night for a short visit. When he did, he would dart across the room to me. I was always the first one he wanted to see.

Bullet was in his thirteenth year when old age caught up with him and he developed an obstruction of the bowels. He survived the operation but died of internal hemorrhaging the following night.

My wife, Elizabeth, was also in the hospital recovering from an operation and still very sick at the time. I wanted to keep the news of Bullet's death from her and the kids until she got better but she asked about Bullet. I had to tell her the truth.

Elizabeth grew up on a farm, too, where the death of animals is part of life. Where a cow is a cow, a chicken is a chicken and a dog is a dog. That's why it surprised me so much when she said that she wanted to bury Bullet in a pet cemetery. It was for the kids, she said, and after all the years of faithful devotion, Bullet deserved it. The alternatives were rather cold and grim for residents in the city, she pointed out.

If anyone had told me before then that I would have spent $350 to bury a dog, I would have said they were crazy. There were too many things we could use that money for.

And a dog is just a dog.

But I gave in, and Bullet was buried in the cemetery in a Styrofoam casket with a planter of flowers on his grave and in between two other dogs who had headstones.

The kids worked hard to find the right words to go on one for Bullet.

That cost me another $150.

We had our own private ceremony for Bullet that day and they put up the headstone later on. My daughter says it's nice. She's been back to see it.

I never have.

Just like I never went back to visit Cap's grave after I got out of service.

Maybe it's because I grew up on a farm where a dog is just a dog.

Or maybe it's because I find it just a little too hard to keep telling old friends goodbye.

ON SONGWRITING

For over twenty years, songwriting was my favorite hobby. Then I decided to pursue it as a small business. After realizing that no one wanted to publish my songs and I was just going to keep on losing money, it became my favorite hobby again. Still is.

I have had a lot of fun writing songs and other writers I have met in the process have been, to the person, nice people. I can say the same thing about the musicians and singers that I have worked with making demonstration tapes of my songs. Of course, I have never met any really successful songwriters yet; but, I bet they're nice people, too.

I have written some songs I am proud of; and, I have tried very hard to get them recorded by someone who could get them on the airwaves where everyone else could enjoy them, too. Unfortunately, I have never been able to get the music publishers or record companies to demonstrate anywhere near that same level of enthusiasm.

Some have said, "It's a nice song, but...

They never say for sure what the "but" is. They would just know it if they heard it.

That's why it's sometimes amusing when someone hears one of my songs for the first time and says, "Hey, that's good! You ought to get George Jones to sing that song for you." You know, just call old Possum up and have him run right over.

I have no idea how many people who want to be songwriters but, from my own limited contacts, there could be millions. That includes, of course, all those club singers in every Holiday Inn, Ramada Inn or other local performance venue in the country who are singing their hearts out every Saturday night while waiting to be discovered. When, and if, that happens, the song that does it, of course, will be one that they've written themselves.

That's why, even though I have won one Honorable Mention and two Top Twenty Five Finalist certificates in four national songwriting contests, I have given up on ever having a breakthrough song myself. But, if anyone is interested, here are a few things I have learned along the way.

The first thing a songwriter needs to do is develop a very thick skin. That comes before talent, craftsmanship or anything. The world is full of critics and when a songwriter solicits other people's opinion of his material, he usually gets it. That's good. That's part of the learning process and, within the right environment, the critiques are professionally given and beneficial. Friends often do not want to dim your enthusiasm or hurt your feelings. Professionals sometimes try to help. That means you do not always hear what you want to hear.

The second most important thing I have learned is that the odds against any top recording artist ever singing one of my songs is pretty slim. Spending a buck on a state lottery ticket may be a better deal; it just isn't as much fun.

But it just may be the quality of my songs that has created that barrier. After all, I have some very nice rejection letters from well-known people in the business. I don't frame my rejection letters, of course, but two are personal, handwritten letters from names you would recognize. And getting anyone with any influence in the music business to listen to your songs is no small feat.

One real problem we amateur songwriters encounter is that we tend to measure our best works against the less than mediocre songs we hear on the radio.

"My song's better than that!" we say, and we're probably right.

But what we are hearing probably isn't a breakthrough song. More likely, it was written by the artist himself or one of his band members or it may have been placed on an album through a song plugger for a publishing company who owed somebody a favor.

The bottom line is that some of the larger publishing companies may have a large number of writers on staff who are being paid a small amount - as an advance against future royalties as I understand the arrangement - to produce a very large volume of songs. If each one of them even had one top fifty hit per year the publishing company would probably be happy. And these people often are talented musicians, some college trained, who are trying valiantly to become professionals.

Even some very small publishers may have a large catalog of songs they actually signed at one time or another -- still unrecorded. Big artists usually don't walk in and listen to them but new artists sometimes do. Say one does. Say your song is on one of those tapes in the publisher's catalog. Say the new artist finds your song out of the thousand there and likes it.

Now the real test comes for that artist to find a recording company who likes both the artist and your song enough to invest big, big bucks into producing, packaging and marketing it.

I once saw boxes of unsolicited tapes sent to a small recording studio that did not, as a rule, record anything other than commercial jingles. I can only imagine how overwhelming the daily inflow of mail must be to legitimate publishers.

On the positive side, music publishers and record companies have a common goal; they both want to hear great songs. But they only spend money to make money; they already have a library full of good songs.

My problem always has been that I thought most of my songs were great; and, I probably wore out my welcome long before I wrote one that might have risen to a higher level than merely good. Sometimes persistence pays off; sometimes it doesn't.

For those with more talent and patience, and who have not yet made all of my mistakes, the resources available on the Internet and through local and national songwriters associations can be useful to aspiring songwriters. Most of my contacts were developed the old fashion way: by obtaining a list of record companies and publishers in the major music centers, using the yellow pages of the telephone directories as a resource. When local libraries did not have the directories, a friendly truck driver seemed to be able to find one on his trips through New York, Los Angeles or Nashville.

Once I had the list, I wrote to those I recognized as legitimate and asked them if they were accepting material. Even then, and with their blessing to send the material, I have had a few envelopes returned with the coldest message on earth stamped on front: "Your unsolicited material is being returned unopened." That's a real bubble buster for any hopeful legend of the music world.

Most of the companies who said they would review the material did review it, in one form or another. They told me how to submit the material, and generally gave me some coded word that will get it past the mailroom. Usually they asked for no more than three songs at a time, accompanied by a lead or lyric sheet and a return postage paid self-addressed envelope if I wanted my material returned. I always noted "Return Postage Enclosed" on the outside of the envelope since I doubted that they would open it otherwise.

The responses I received from my initial inquiries also helped in other ways. The correspondent might indicate what type of material they were looking for or the artist they are representing and how long I could expect to wait before I heard from them. It could be six months or a year.

Others have, in declining to receive the material, provided me with advice as to how to get my songs reviewed by legitimate interests without being victimized by "song sharks," or those illegitimate concerns that prey on the hopes and dreams of unsophisticated amateurs.

Even when I got the invitation to submit material, it was still hard to tell what the publisher really wanted to hear. Some would say they needed only a vocal backed by a single instrument; they would be able to envision or "hear" the final arrangement.

I know one writer, though, who said that he and a patron backer had spent a large sum of money on a demonstration tape for a song that all of us who heard it thought was beautiful. He also had the good fortune of being personally acquainted with members of a very successful musical group who got him an audition with the arrangement and recording director of their record company, a major label. When the A&R man heard the tape, he said: "Nice song. Let me hear it again when you get it finished."

I think that one of the problems, too, is that some publishers and record companies receive so much material that they have to hire people to listen to the songs and screen them for someone else. One such person told me that he had so many to screen that he would only listen to a brief snippet of the tape, if at all, and gave preference to songs from people whose name he recognized. Thus, the unworthy would be culled from the stack with only a few seconds of sound. If he was not "hooked" in that few seconds enough to listen to some more of it, the song was dead.

About hooks: "If I said you had a beautiful body, would you hold it against me," and "If you're going to do me wrong, do it right." are two of my favorites. I don't have any that even come close.

But in spite of my own lack of success, others have crossed the bar. I was always encouraged by stories such as how Tom T. Hall, known as the great storyteller, carried around "Harper Valley P.T.A." for a year or so before he could get anyone interested. And how Kris Kristofferson - in my opinion, one of the best songwriters of my time - got Johnny Cash to hear "Sunday Morning Coming Down." The stories may even be true.

These people and others like them were making the big sacrifices. They were at the scene, surviving as best they could, living to be songwriters. They, of course, had the talent and persistence to succeed. Many others have made similar sacrifices and did not succeed. I'm glad I chose to make my living some other way.

But, to be truthful about it, I have been told by some nice, but knowledgeable people, that while they admire my talent, my songs are simply too traditional or old fashioned. I think that means I have been writing songs all these years for dead singers. But, there's that old saying, whatever goes around, comes around; and, heck, I'm old but I still have time - if they hurry.

I guess all of this is why songwriting is still my favorite hobby.

There have been highlights, of course. Not too long ago, I had a compilation made of five of my songs that had been produced in Nashville and recorded by a young singer, Rachel Coogle, who is a tremendous vocal talent. Then, a friend of mine, Ray Beaufait, saw the CD and heard the songs. I didn't know it at the time but Ray has a successful web site, Beauproductions, from

Rachel Coogle

*Glass Slippers
And Paper Back Dreams*

which he sells a variety of excellent multimedia CD's that he also produces. He wanted to add Rachel's CD to his site. After only a day or so, we sold the first copy. We remained a number one seller for over two weeks. Then we sold number two.

I know the site was being visited, though, because I received an inquiry from a disk jockey in Austria, wanting some promotional material on Rachel. Her manager sent a complete portfolio and I watched the DJ's web site to see if her name ever appeared on his published play list. It finally did and one Sunday afternoon, Rachel's beautiful voice was lilting across the Austrian countryside - singing somebody else's song.

The business I mentioned earlier was a single record a friend and I backed on a song we co-wrote. It got some local airplay but that was it. Still, it was fun hearing my song being played right up there on the radio with Kenny Rogers and Barbara Mandrel.

Another thing that I've enjoyed, too, is the performances of my songs by some of the local entertainers who have done some demonstration work for me. One song that I wrote for Elizabeth for our twenty-fifth wedding anniversary, received a number of requests by Al Henderson who did the demo. And when Elizabeth and I visited Al's club, he usually introduced Elizabeth to the patrons telling them I wrote the song for her and then would perform it, beautifully, as the dance floor filled.

Elizabeth was always so proud. So was I.

Songwriting can be a lot of fun if you don't get too serious about it. If you do, it can break your heart.

ON GARAGE SALES

I think that garage sales can provide some of the most fun - and frustration - a person can have. Where else can someone dispose of a year's accumulation of surplus items, deriving both cash and a tax deduction for the residue at the same time? The old saying, "One man's junk is another man's treasure", is never more meaningful than at a garage sale.

The frustration comes in at times like when I was helping Elizabeth with her cash box and a man came up wanting to pay two dollars for a barely used golf pull cart of mine, priced at a measly five dollars. I really wasn't anxious to part with that golf cart - especially at that price - and it ticked me off a little that he was trying to steal it. I may not have been my normal, jovial self as I declined his offer and he walked away. However, in a few minutes he came back, willing to pay the full five dollars. During the brief time he was gone, a lady had come by and bought the cart, happy to have made such a terrific purchase. I dutifully expressed my regrets to the man, of course. Part frustration; part fun.

While I am not an expert on the garage sale phenomenon myself, I can claim to be a beneficiary. My sister, Ruth, who lived in central Indiana, bought me an antique smoke stand and

a beautiful old violin, both acquired dirt cheap, which I consider priceless. Some of my own discarded possessions no doubt have received similar favor somewhere else. That's the way garage sales work.

Elizabeth used to have a garage sale almost every year. She would clean out the basement and the closets of all unused articles and mark them for sale. Then the kids and I would come along and remove things we didn't even remember we owned, but which were suddenly too precious to part with. That usually cut the inventory at least in half. Aside from selling unused items for a little money, there is a distinct pleasure in seeing some needy families acquire useful "throwaways" at bargain prices. At one of our sales, one older gentleman bought a perfectly good set of premium tires for his pickup truck for ten dollars. Many families have clothed their children in fashionable, but outgrown, designer jeans and blouses at a fraction of their cost. That's making sense out of cents.

Following one of Elizabeth's garage sales; however, a lady brought an item back. It was my son's long outgrown winter jacket he had when he was three or four years old. She wasn't asking for a refund. The coat was so cute and in such beautiful condition that she thought Charlie, our son, might want to keep it as a memento of his childhood.

In the modern world, where recycling is a recurring buzzword, where better to begin than at a garage sale like this one? A successful lawyer, who is a friend of mine, had a garage sale when he moved out of his larger home into a condominium. He needed to reduce the amount of furnishings he had and didn't want to store them or go through an auction. His wife became totally involved in the project and even ended up selling more items than they intended to sell. "I've never seen anyone as excited," he said, "about selling ten thousand dollars worth of furniture for five hundred dollars!"

Situations such as his produce bargains without any stigma of a handout. Both the poor and not so poor frequent them and all somehow enjoy and benefit from them. A lot of things Elizabeth has purchased at garage sales have ended up in her own next sale.

I guess the real thrill is finding a bargain; not keeping it. Besides, there's no storage space left.

That's why we were having the garage sale in the first place.

ON MOTIVATION

You could hear Willie coming long before he made the turn around the bend of that old dusty country road. His cheerful whistling would cut through the bushes and cross the creek like an advance trumpeter. And when he finally sauntered into view, you always wondered how anyone could whistle that fast and walk that slow.

Willie was never in a hurry. When he passed by, he would always stop to visit. Not on the porch or in the house but there on the road, hunkered down on his haunches in a way I've only seen mountain men do - which is as close to sitting down as you can get without getting your pants wet.

It is an art, I suspect, perfected during the early morning hours on some dew-drenched mountain, watching up through the trees for a gray squirrel to come out of his nest.

Willie could sit that way for hours, just passing the time and talking about almost anything in that easy, friendly way of his. He was one of those genuinely likeable people who you naturally enjoyed being around.

And now and then, Willie would even hire out to you as a field hand for maybe a day or two at a time. But other than that, and putting out a small garden in the spring and harvesting whatever happened to grow in the fall, Willie never worked.

That's why it came as such a shock when I heard that Willie was dead. They said he was killed by a slate fall in a small truck mine over in Buchanan County, Virginia along with a friend of his.

Christmas time was coming on and Willie apparently had found a job so he could buy his boys a bicycle for Christmas. I guess his love for his boys finally did what nothing else had ever done; put Willie to work. But, from what I was told, Willie never even saw his first paycheck. He was on the job less than two weeks when the slate fall halted his unusual surge of ambition - forever.

Willie's family came out fine financially. There was Social Security, some miners' benefits and even a cash settlement from somewhere. They were able to build on to their little two-room cabin and some of the kids even went on through high school. His widow remarried and a new garden got planted every spring. Life goes on.

Such subtleties of personal motivation come back to me when I think about the day my daughter got her driver's license. Sharon had passed the driving part of the test in a high school driver's education class and needed only to pass the written part of the exam. I didn't go in with her but the broad smile on her face told me she had passed the test just as soon as she opened the door.

I offered to let her drive home just to test out her new license, but she didn't want to. She said she was too nervous.

The fact is, she didn't drive for almost a year after that. She apparently believed that the instructor had passed her on the driving part out of the goodness of his heart; and, she was totally content with the situation as it was. Her goal was to have the driver's license, not to drive.

But several months later she needed some hair spray - a crisis in any teenage girl's life - and there was no one to take her to the store. She went out and got in the car and has been driving ever since.

I have read a lot of books on motivation, listened to many audiotapes and attended several inspiring seminars. Most of them were of the "one size fits all" variety designed for the highly charged world of commerce. They would not have motivated Willie to get a job or Sharon to drive before they had their own reason to. That had to come from inside. For Sharon, motivation was a can of hair spray; for Willie, it was a bicycle for his boys. The things that motivate people are as different as the people themselves.

When the more highly promoted external motivational techniques are used, they can fail miserably when a person is encouraged to do something he really doesn't want, or isn't ready, to do. Sometimes a capable person is taken from a job or situation which provides perfect contentment and persuaded, in the interest of advancement, to assume responsibilities for which he or she is not mentally prepared. In my experience, what happens next is often tragic unless there is understanding and a good relationship involved.

Discontentment grows and the qualities that made the person, attractive as a promotional candidate, dissolve into a sea of unmet expectations. But whose expectations?

I often have wondered what happened to a young lady - introduced to me as a highly competent new hire and richly deserving of her challenging position - who was being indoctrinated by a client I was visiting one morning. The only thing I remember about his conversation with her is his admonition, "I won't come down on you if. . ." What unnecessary baggage that must have been to carry around with her on the first exciting day of her new job.

While motivation can take better forms and is extremely useful when properly administered, it is important to know and understand the person to whom it is being directed. Sometimes a nurturing environment, more than the practiced eloquence of motivational speeches, is all it takes. It has always been somewhat of a contradiction to me that people who believe so strongly that "cream rises" think they always have to be stirring up the milk.

If we open the door, provide encouragement and opportunity; and, establish an understandable level of expectations and values, I believe that the cream will rise on its own.

If we churn it with constant pressure - the form of motivation chosen by so many - we often end up with buttermilk.

There is an important maturation process involved which contains its own compelling truth: A person needs time to grow; to develop skills and confidence. Unfortunately, not all of them will.

The important elements are access and opportunity; the drivers license in the purse of a teenage girl. Sooner or later, if the confidence grows to the right level, she will know she can drive. Then, given the right reason, she will fulfill her own expectations and, perhaps, ours in the process.

That's why, I suppose, that the memory of Willie stays with me; not as a tragic irony of life but as a statement on life itself.

There is a natural eagerness among all of us to give ourselves credit for having been a source of inspiration and motivation to others in the pursuit of their life and career goals. But it is a one sided scoreboard. Our failures fade just as easily from our memory. They become the spilled milk that's not worth crying over.

Even in its most modest form, success always seems to be shared. Not so with failure. Failures bear the burden by themselves.

ON HOMEPLACES

They say that, from the time she first saw it, my mother always wanted to live in that house.

Or maybe it was where the house was.

It was just an old faded white clapboard farm house but it set on its own gently rolling plateau with a wide front porch overlooking the river and the field beyond, which stretched over to the main road.

You could sit on the front porch and see who was going somewhere that day or you could look down on the people in the few old shanties an eighth of a mile below. Maybe that was the source of her dream. Maybe she wanted to look down on someone else for a change.

Dad managed to rent the house, later using the insurance money from their eldest son's death during World War II to buy the place.

He moved her into it during the last few months of her relatively young life. I'm not sure she knew Paul was missing in action at the time. It would have hurt deeply.

She had loved all of her eleven children. Seven were born before the Depression when the family was reasonably well off and could afford them. Fortunes change and the harder life had taken its toll.

My mother died at home in the front bedroom from the last of a series of strokes. My older sister sent my little brother and me out into the orchard where we waited until the undertaker could be contacted and brought in to take care of things.

I was only seven and Ethan three years younger and neither of us really knew what was going on. I found myself crying mostly because everyone else was and my little brother cried because I did.

My memories of that day otherwise remain hazy which, I suppose, is God's way of insulating children from such tragedies so early in life.

I suppose that the reason and the way we got our home place were the roots of my father's attachment to it. He would also live out his days there, outliving another wife and son in the process, and it would be the place where my little brother and I grew into manhood.

I never really appreciated the beauty of our land until I saw it through someone else's eyes several years later.

It extended from the road, across a field, over the river, up the rise to the house and then beyond the orchard, meadow and poplar groves to the mountain.

From the top of the mountain in winter, a boy could ride a sled down the logging trails, gathering enough speed to take him across all the meadows and fields, under barbed wire fences, down the side road, across the bridge and on to the main road only to eventually lose all momentum on the hills of the road itself. It took an hour or two to get to the top of the mountain and only a few minutes to come down.

But it was worth it for the ride.

The river that ran through the place wasn't really a river now that I know what a river is. But it seemed too big to be called a creek or a stream. Its width probably ranged from twenty-five to one hundred fifty feet and I doubt that it was deeper than five or six feet at its deepest parts except during spring floods.

Then it did become a river, whatever it was before; and, when it washed out the bridges, we had to walk almost a mile through the woods to get to the main road. If it had been a creek or a stream we would have waded it instead of walking through those woods after dark, without a light or a gun, and knowing what was out there in those trees.

The bobcats or wildcats were what I feared most. I have lain in bed at night and heard them crying from the edge of the orchard. It makes you pull the covers a little tighter around you and grateful that your dogs are outside on the porch.

In the summer, though, the river was our principal source of pleasure. It provided a cool, refreshing escape at the end of a hard, hot day when the swimming hole would become a gathering place for all the kids around.

It was also a place to practice with a rifle, shooting water snakes off the willow trees as they lay sunning themselves. A good shot meant that there was one less snake to confront while you were swimming or grappling for fish under the rocks in the shoals. We would pole a homemade raft up the river and ride it back down. It was like shooting at a moving target except we were doing the moving.

The river was also a source of food and, during those times my brother and I had to fend for ourselves, we could go down to the river, catch a fish and scale it and fry it for breakfast. Otherwise, we might have to wait for a hen to lay an egg and you can get pretty hungry doing that.

In fact, a person had to be lazy or ignorant to starve on our place, from the things growing wild. Water cress, plantain and polk stalks; apples, peaches and pears; hickory nuts and walnuts; mulberries, blackberries, plums, cherries and paw paws; rabbits, squirrels and pheasants: the variety was endless.

Or there was wild mint and rabbit tobacco, "life everlasting" as we called it, if you wanted something to chew on your way to hunt the cow. But if you didn't find her, that was okay. She would be back when she needed milking. Cows are smarter than a lot of people that way; they always seem to know when its time to go home.

I never went home often enough but sometimes, when I look back at the old home place, I'm glad I grew up there. It taught me self-sufficiency and gave me a certain degree of independence. But I didn't love it like my father and, in spite of all the practice, I never shared his enthusiasm for the gardens, cornfields or forestry. To him, it was a labor of love; to me it was just labor.

Dad's concern for growing things still lacked focus to me even when I reached my mid teens and began to question why we always seemed to raise more corn than we could ever use. I got up the courage to ask him one night at supper. He said we raised the corn to feed the horse. Then I asked him why we kept the horse. He had already answered, "To raise the corn," before that look came across his face. That fall, he sold the horse but several years later, when he died, it was out there in his garden pushing a wheel plow, still trying to make things grow.

When I returned home for Dad's funeral, I took my own young son out to the orchard where I had been with my little brother so many years before when my mother died. And I think it was then, sitting there with Charlie and reflecting on my own life on the old home place that the realization finally hit me. Dad never really was raising corn; he was raising kids. With him gone and my own four year old beside me, I knew whose turn it was now.

It was many years before I went back home after Dad died. In the interim, the place eventually sold for back taxes – a difficult situation resulting from my father having died without a will and leaving a wife, stepchildren and, therefore, a cloudy title to the land. My brother, Darrell, and I talked about bidding it in ourselves - which either of us could have easily afforded to do - just to keep it in the family. We decided not to for reasons better left to him and me.

That farm was my mother's dream and my father's love. It raised her young children to manhood and gave us a place to go back to when there were cobwebs to clear from the mind or to visit with Dad and scattered members of the family once or twice a year. The cobwebs come back from time to time but all of the other reasons are gone.

It was a good place but it had served its purpose.

The old house has been torn down and a modern bi-level now sets on its site. It turned out that a very good friend of my father had bought the farm, did extensive excavating and landscaping and turned it in to a show place in that area. Except for a barn and some old outbuildings, it is a different place. A home place, now, for someone else.

The house never really made any difference; it was always the land that was important. And no one ever really "owns" a place. If they hold title, they just get to use it on their way through life. If they take care of it, it will take care of them.

But my mother's, my father's and my time at our old home place had passed. It didn't need us anymore.

ON ROUTE 66

Sometime during 1951, my junior year in high school, an older sister talked me into going to California with her and her husband. There were jobs out there that were better than anything her husband, Stanley, could find in West Virginia and she apparently wanted me along for the company.

Marie had been to California before and the picture she painted - along with my own desire to see what was beyond the mountains - persuaded me to go. In many ways, it was the trip of a lifetime; in other ways it was a lifetime of a trip.

Soon after we arrived at our destination, San Bernardino, I was enrolled in school and in my first class, on my first day, the teacher told me that the class assignment was to present a talk about "favorite authors." She thought that since I was new in class and was certain to already know something about my favorite author, perhaps I should go first. Bear in mind that I had just arrived there from a small town in West Virginia where the population of the entire town was only thirteen hundred and dropped into a school with an enrollment of over three thousand on a campus containing thirteen buildings. Then, while still dumbfounded by everything I had experienced from the five day trip to get to this new world, all she wanted me to do was get up in front of a big room of total strangers and tell them what little I knew about Jack London. How I managed to get through that day is still regarded as a minor miracle in my life.

But I digress.

We left West Virginia in a 1947 Kaiser on an afternoon and Stanley drove all night. Somewhere during that time I had gone to sleep and when I woke up, we were nearing Cairo, Illinois where we would cross the Mississippi. I had completely missed the Kentucky bluegrass in the darkness and was highly disappointed. At the time, I thought it really was blue.

I don't remember when or how often Stanley took brief naps, but he stopped as infrequently as possible. It is obvious to me now that he didn't have much money so restaurants and leisurely sight seeing were out of the question. Gasoline, water and parts for the car, when needed, were the top priorities.

Although it was crowded with boxes and bags of things we would need, I had the rest of the back seat of that old Kaiser all to myself. I stayed busy taking in all the new and wondrous sights along the way. That was the first time I recall seeing the Burma Shave advertising signs that used to dot the highway. They were positioned just far enough apart to let you read their continuing message as you anticipated the next line. One read, in five parts: His line was smooth / But not his chin / He took her out / She took him in / To buy some Burma Shave.

The first really mind boggler, though, was when we crossed the Mississippi River. I never dreamed that any river could be that wide. Through the mist you could see big boats going up and down the river and it conjured up memories of Tom Sawyer and Huckleberry Finn. That's when, I guess, that the rivers back home, where we rode our puny little homemade rafts, suddenly became creeks and streams.

I'm not sure where we finally connected with Route 66 but it was somewhere in Missouri. It was still a two-lane blacktop road but you could tell, immediately, that there was something special about it. Its markings were clearer, its asphalt was blacker, and its shoulders were wider than anything we had driven on in West Virginia or Kentucky. This was the Mother Road; it would run through parts of Missouri, Kansas, Oklahoma, Texas, New Mexico, Arizona and California. All we had to do now was follow its route signs and it would take us all the way to the Promised Land.

Driving Route 66 meant that you passed through, not around, every city and town on the map along the way. Each one added its own traffic delays but muted that minor inconvenience with a variety of visual attractions. There was a strange and inexplicable beauty to the ever changing scenery: restaurants and motels inviting you to look inside their wigwam or other unusual shapes and forms; neon signs barking their wares in grand and boisterous fashion; wind mills sucking the last drop of moisture from the earth.

Mile after mile, day after day, it was the adventure of a lifetime. Wheat fields gave way to oil fields which gave way to ranch land where real live cowboys worked their real live cattle herds across an endless landscape. We passed through places with names like Amarillo, Tucumcari, Albuquerque, Flagstaff and Needles. Along the way, we saw deserts and mountains, presenting themselves in unique forms and colors, and the occasional hut or wickiup of the Indians - Native Americans as they are called now - who somehow survived on a severe and barren land. We also saw more than a few junkyards filled with the carcasses of old cars that had lost their battle with the road.

Then came the real adventure.

I never knew any place could be as hot or dry or long or desolate as the Mojave Desert. And, without air conditioning or other modern comforts, it seemed like we would never reach the mountains even though we could see them from miles away. Then, when we did, a blizzard had closed the road at Cajon Pass to all cars except those with chains. Being from West Virginia, we had a pair in the trunk and were able to go on.

Imagine leaving behind a mountain pass closed by snow and then descending into a valley filled with warm sun and orange groves. (Beyond that, at a later date, the Pacific Ocean.) That's pretty heady stuff for a sixteen-year old mountain boy.

It would take another book and a much sharper memory to cover all the wonders of traveling Route 66 back in the fifties. The road is gone now, of course, except for parts kept open by historical interests. But I rode it, all the way from Missouri to California - the Mother Road for all those seeking escape from whatever caused them to leave their homes back east, looking for a better life in the golden promised land.

My promise there was short lived, unfortunately, since I had to return home the following school year in order to graduate from high school on time. The California school system required two years of a foreign language and, at that point in time and where I was from, one could question my ability to speak my own native tongue.

But I cherish that trip and those memories and I share the sense of loss with so many others now that this important piece of Americana history is gone. My short time on the old Route 66, and what it lead me to, was long and hard; but, boy oh boy! I wouldn't have missed it for the world!

ON GOLF

A few years ago, while on vacation in South Carolina, I was watching show host Arthur Smith on regional television. The guest was country singer Webb Pierce. During his interview, Smith asked Pierce if he had any special interests or hobbies outside of his music. Pierce said "No, not really. I tried to play a little golf one time but I found out I wasn't any good at it."

"That's great!" Smith replied, "I've known some people who have played for years and haven't learned that yet."

Arthur Smith wasn't talking about me but he could have been. I used to be a golf addict and have a ski suit to prove it. My wife bought it for me to wear in sub-freezing weather after she had finally concluded that my judgment, like my golf score, wasn't likely to improve.

It wasn't that I didn't try; golf is simply like playing a guitar. Anyone can play it poorly but few ever learn to play really well. That's because golf isn't really a game, it's applied physics. But even a degree in engineering wouldn't help you master all the scientific principles required to really play it well. The pro's just got lucky.

Consider, for example, all the clubs suggested for the bag, each of which is intended to advance the ball from tee to green. These are principally the woods, irons, pitching wedge and a putter--except the woods may be made out of aluminum, magnesium or something else and the irons aren't really iron either.

The good thing about it all is that so called "natural athletes" may not have any particular advantage. That's because golf is an "unnatural" game. Just watch the guy who is five-foot-six out drive the guy who is six-foot-five.

But, back to the clubs. Each one is intended for a specific purpose or distance. The distance for which each is used depends on the individual player and how well he or she has mastered the swing. I have learned exactly how far I can hit any club in my bag. With either a driver or a nine iron, I can hit in the middle of the nearest water hazard, sand trap or immediately behind the loneliest tree in the fairway.

I don't feel badly about that. Just remember all of the golf advice and lessons you've ever had. Now, mentally address the ball. Carefully align yourself with the target; feet shoulder width apart with the left foot slightly toed out. Place the ball comfortably at arms length anywhere from the inside of your left foot to the middle of your stance, depending on which club you selected. Stick your butt out slightly and flex your knees so that the club head will barely meet the ground at impact. Remember, of course, to keep your eye on the ball, your head still and your left arm straight. Pull the club head away slowly in a backward movement, turning the hips as the arms raise the club upward to the top of its arc. You're now half way home.

As you start your downswing, shift your hip leftward out of the way, turning the body as you pull the club head through the ball with your left arm. Continue the follow-through upward to a full swing, turning so that your belly button is now facing the target. Now you can look up. If you can see the ball anywhere except still on the tee, good job! If you can't see it, begin searching in the next fairway. You meet an awful lot of nice people that way.

Of course if you are left handed, reverse all of the above and pull through with the right arm. But the ball is still in the next fairway, it's just on the other side.

If all that sounds like a contradiction, that's how golf is. Left-handed people use their right arm. The harder you try to hit the ball, the shorter the distance you get. And a golf ball will roll away from the hole on the slightest incline but will stick solidly on a steep incline if it happens to be under the overhang of a sand trap. I've known some golfers who carried little cheat sheets in their pocket just to remember these things.

Another good thing to know is that golf balls are better than divining rods or witching sticks for finding water. And water, any little trickle of

water, on a golf course can turn the nerviest combat veteran into jelly. You can tell it from the bravado as they step up to the ball.

"The last time I put a ball in the water this close was in World War II."

They even use their shining new Blue Max instead of one of the old cut balls in their bag just to show you how confident they are. Then they address the ball, feet shoulder width apart, knees slightly flexed, butt stuck out, take their swing and listen for the fatal sound.

Kerplunk!

It all adds new truth to that old expression: Old golfers never die; they just lose their balls.

If the situation gets too frustrating, a golfer can blame it on his golf clubs--too old, too new, too stiff, too much flex--or on his golf shoes, bad lie, his wife, or anything else that comes to his addled mind.

If a golfer wants to improve, he can practice a lot after a lesson or two from his club professional. I went to one to improve my skill with a driver. He started me on the short irons to "groove" my swing. I did okay the first lesson because I could already hit the short irons, but after that I got progressively worse. He didn't even charge me for the fifth lesson. I never touched a wood through all five lessons and I still can't hit a driver. But my iron play is coming back.

I have seen some miraculous things on a golf course. I've even made a hole-in-one, almost made another and holed a dribbled tee shot that I slugged in disgust in an angry walk toward the green. But there are two others you won't believe.

One happened in a game with my brother-in-law, Ron, who I introduced to golf and who has beaten me consistently ever since. I finally had him by one stroke on the last hole at Jenny Wiley when I hit my tee shot straight down the fairway and he hooked into the woods. His second shot out of the trees hit the visitors' center roof, rolled down the drainpipe, across the pavement, down the hill and on to the green. My second shot didn't even come close. You know what they say about old golfers.

The other was something I saw and still don't believe. The guy I was playing with hit a pitch shot just off the green. I saw the swing out of the corner of my eye but it was the blood coming from a cut on his nose that really drew my attention. He said that he dropped the club and it hit a rock or something, and bounced back up to hit his nose. I don't blame him; I saw it and I wouldn't have admitted it either. But, personally, I think he'll make a great golfer someday. Golf is, indeed, a scientific game and torque is important. I say that anyone with enough body torque to cut himself in the nose, swinging a pitching wedge, has to be able to drive any par four around, once he gets that little control problem straightened out.

Anyway, I don't play much golf anymore. I took a long time off a few years back when I cracked a rib trying to hit a five wood two hundred and fifty yards. That could have been the best stroke I've ever taken in my life. While my mind still wants to remember that, my body just can't seem to take it anymore.

But as frustrating or painful as golf can be, as humiliating or expensive, it's hard to stay away from it. That's because we like to think of golf as a one-man sport. Regardless of how badly our playing partners beat us, we tell ourselves we're really playing against the course. And we know, deep down inside, we're better than how we played today. For our own peace of mind we have to be.

Which leads to my final and firmest belief about golf: Every golfer will hit at least one magnificent golf shot on either the sixteenth, seventeenth or eighteenth hole. That's so he'll have one to remember.

So he'll keep on coming back.

ON NEIGHBORHOODS

In nearly fifty years of marriage, Elizabeth and I have lived in eight different neighborhoods. We have liked them all. If that is reminiscent of Will Roger's commentary on the men he had met, that's understandable; the reasons are pretty much the same.

The first three places we lived don't count. They were all in my wife's hometown where the people are always friendly to the home folks. The real test came in Lexington, Kentucky, our first move away from home.

Although we rented a duplex in a mixed commercial and residential neighborhood, it wasn't bad. In fact, one of my favorite memories comes from there; more specifically, from the neighbors in the other unit of the duplex. Curt and Leona were married, for the second or third time each, after we moved in.

For the first few months, they were a loving and friendly couple. Then Leona started appearing frail and sickly, complaining regularly of one ailment or another. She apparently started feeding Curt TV dinners on almost a regular basis. Before their separation, she came over crying one night following a loud disturbance we had been wondering about. Curt had thrown his TV dinner against the wall in an impolite protest. Leona's description of the spaghetti sliding down the wall remains vivid in my mind.

Our next stop was Murfreesboro, Tennessee. Murfreesboro was a nice southern town with a courthouse square. There were not many jobs available for men but the new factories in town offered piecework to women with sewing skills. In the summer, some of the local men would congregate on the park benches outside the courthouse and whittle all day long. In the winter they would go inside. Locally, they were called "Go Getters." They would take their wives to work at the factories in the morning; come back to the courthouse to spend their days; and, then, at quitting time, they would "go get 'er."

Murfreesboro was a friendly town and I was grateful. My wife and baby were young and I had to travel quite a bit, leaving them home alone. The neighbors looked out for them and we really hated to leave when my promotion came. But this was a significant move to Louisville, Kentucky - home office of my company.

Actually we moved to Jeffersonville, Indiana right across the Ohio River. We knew some people there and that made moving more comfortable.

But we were warned: don't expect the people to be as friendly here.

Our first house was rented temporarily until we had our home built. We only lived there six months but by the time we left, I think my wife knew everyone on the street. Some of them still talk of the pretty young woman with the cute southern accent who used to call for her son when he was outside playing. Elizabeth was never shy.

She took that same extroverted, trusting quality to our new neighborhood where we lived for over thirty years. In less than six months, neighbors who never knew each other were having coffee at our kitchen table. Most of the friendships formed in those years have endured and even those who have moved away still return, treating Elizabeth like a sister.

When I think about it, I am reminded again of Murfreesboro, Tennessee and the man who owned the Ben Franklin store on the courthouse square. One day as I was passing by, he was just concluding a conversation with a stranger. I stopped to visit and he told me that the man he was talking to was just moving into town. He wanted to know if Murfreesboro was a friendly place. The storeowner had asked him how people were where he came from. "Not too friendly," the stranger had said. The storeowner told him he would probably find them the same way here.

I personally do not have all that many friends. Elizabeth has a lot. We always seem to have been blessed with living in a friendly neighborhood.

ON PREJUDICE

We had only one black person in my hometown. His name was Jim and he rode around on a bicycle with a guitar strapped around his neck. He lived in the train station, where he worked, but at night he always appeared at the Dirty Shame saloon where he would entertain the patrons for drinks.

I had never come into personal contact with any African Americans, or blacks, until I joined the Army. I suppose this was the ultimate reflection of prejudice somewhere along the line but I had never really thought about it that way. The only ones I had ever seen, other than Jim, were through a Greyhound bus window passing through other towns.

In the service, though, I met Washington. He was from Virginia and he was just an ordinary, nice, humble person like most of the people I had known. He made a little extra money during basic training by washing and ironing the clothes of some of the people who could afford it. I had to wash my own; that's how I got to know Washington.

We didn't get a pass until our last week of basic training. Three or four of us were going into Louisville and we invited Washington along. All of us were from small towns and none of us knew anything about Louisville, so we went to the U.S.O., the United Services Organization, which catered to servicemen.

They let all of us in, except Washington. They said there was a black club down the street where he could go. We started to argue about the exclusion but Washington told us not to. He had seen all this before and he knew we hadn't. He just left.

We shot pool and passed the time but all of us had sort of an empty feeling about what happened to Washington. Things were never quite the same after that.

Several years later, in Murfreesboro, Tennessee, my two year old son was standing in our back yard silently peering at another two year old on the other side of the fence. It was a little black boy who had crossed the long field between his house and ours.

They didn't say anything; they just stared at each other.

When my son came into the house he must have recognized a difference between him and the other boy because he had asked: "Mommy, what kind of children is that?"

I never thought of myself as prejudiced but I grew up in a town where blacks apparently were not welcome. When Washington could not stay at the white USO, I did. And when our son asked us about the little boy across the fence, I'm not sure we gave him the right answer.

To my knowledge, no member of my family, no matter how far back you could trace the branches of the tree, ever owned a slave. All the time I was growing up, there was never any evidence of racial prejudice since there was no one of color around, except Jim - who, as far as I know, was liked by everyone - to be prejudiced against. But my own life experiences have provided ample proof that it exists. And it isn't just a matter of black and white. Nor, after more than a hundred years, can it all be tied to slavery anymore. Those who are perpetuating prejudice are doing so to accomplish their own agenda; however right, wrong, simple or complicated that may be.

Sometimes I feel that I'm in the middle of something I didn't start and something far beyond my power to end.

Sometimes I'm not sure there is an end.

ON KNOWLEDGE

As human beings, our most potentially fatal weakness can be summed up simply: We don't know what we don't know. I say this with the hindsight of many experiences, one of the most painful of which having occurred in a moderately high stakes (for me at least) seven card stud game where I lost four natural sevens to four natural eights. Up until that time it had been my night; there were two or three wild players in the game and I was playing on several hundred dollars of their money. The game was winding down when I hit a gambler's dream: four of a kind on the first four cards; two sevens up and two in the hole. Nobody paid much attention to my modest pair so I laid back in the weeds, with a lock on the board, letting them build the pot. On the sixth card I started to push. They figured I had paired one of my hole cards.

I had been watching the table all along but after the seventh card, one of the players called a healthy bet and my raise and then raised himself. I took an even better look at his hand after that. He had a possible straight flush showing but it had been broken at the high end and I had his seven in the hole.

He had also been playing desperately toward the end of the game because he was the game's heavy loser. I was sure he had a straight or a flush but the best I could possibly see was a concealed full house. I raised him back.

One eight up and three eights in the hole! If anyone had a right to catch the case eight on the last card, I guess he did. I still walked away a winner but it sure didn't feel that way. Not when you go down with a "lock" on the board.

Some people nowadays would say my problem was that I didn't "look outside the box." The real problem - and theirs, too, I suppose - is that I never seemed to know when I was in a box. That takes vision; not knowledge. Some have it; some don't.

In life, as in poker, if we knew the true level of our intelligence, or ignorance, we could look for better answers to our problems. Instead we can only rely upon the limited knowledge already stored within the framework of our own personal experience. That can be comforting at times, when our success as decision-makers generally depends so much upon being right.

Sometimes we see the results with its full glory or devastation. But too often we may never know if the decision we made was the best; we know only if it turned out good or bad. Old adages protect us from any speculation. "There's no use crying over spilled milk." "Hindsight has twenty-twenty vision." You've heard them all.

But in my honest opinion, most decisions are instinctive or intuitive and are all self-serving in one form or another. Usually, however, they are couched in some type of language which illustrates their good for the shareholders, their good for the community or whatever other praiseworthy good for something that conceals this ancillary truth.

Obviously, many decisions are good for all concerned and that is when the decision maker really comes out smelling like a rose. I am sure I have often made less than the "best" decision because of the limitations of my own experience or for personal gain, which I would never consciously accept or admit. But, of course, that is only my opinion and no one should ever rely upon that. That's because I view these decisions from my own level of knowledge within my own small frame of reference.

During my lifetime, I have had the benefit of many learning experiences. These have ranged from curving a cue ball to creating corporate mergers. I've even had the privilege of teaching college level courses in business and have been a student, myself, in a wide variety of other subjects. Yet, in the total body of knowledge of the world's population, what I know would not fill a pinhead. I've learned, however, to not spend a lot of time pondering how bare my cupboard of knowledge really is. The digestive system works better that way.

In poker, you should know there are four eights out there somewhere. In life, things don't usually come in such neat sets. You never know for certain what the other guy has in the hole.

That's why I say it sure would be a lot easier if I knew what it is that I don't know. That's not from a lack of people who like to tell me; it's my own fault. I'm always afraid they may be in the same boat. Even though they may act like they know it all, somehow I'm never sure they really do.

ON TRAFFIC

My wife has a terrible time getting me out of the house for anything anymore. She thinks its because I hate crowds, which is partially true. I have developed a real aversion to exchanging bone-crushing blows and body fragrances with total strangers on hot summer days, regardless of the attraction that brought us all together. But that is a lesser reason.

Wherever I seem to go anymore, there are other people who want to go there too. And a lot of them are going places I don't even want to go. So maybe crowds aren't the problem after all. Maybe it's that never ending stream of cars, some with noticeable homicidal intent, that move us to those places of mass congregation.

If you go to a major sporting event, just wait until you're ready to leave. The real competition is outside in the parking lot. A person would be better off saving the price of the ticket and just sitting out there watching the people scramble for position in the exit lanes. Life is cheap.

Unfortunately, the same thing happens everywhere else. I've seen some people who seem willing to kill to get into the closest parking space to the entrance to a shopping mall, and then walk for a mile once they get inside. It becomes a game. As you politely and patiently wait for a driver backing out of his parking space, in zooms someone from the opposite direction. "Gotcha!" say's the expression on their face. A real competitive spirit. And, again, that's only in parking lots.

Sometimes in traffic you see things happening you don't believe; like the little old lady who sat through a green light waiting for an arrow so she can make a right turn.

Or the man in Chattanooga who hit me from the rear. I saw it coming in my rear view mirror while we were stopped at the red light. He turned around to slap the kids in the back seat and unconsciously took his foot off the brake. He was extremely apologetic and noticeably frustrated. It was a hot day and he had driven all the way from Alabama with three or four small children. His wife apparently couldn't control them. I don't know where he was going but, wherever it was, it must have been too far on only one set of nerves.

Another time in Tennessee, I had a semi behind me on a mountain going down a long, curvy two-lane road with only narrow, rocky shoulders. He was right on my bumper, blowing his horn for me to speed up or get out of the way. I grew up on mountain roads and to stay out of his way I exceeded all reason to keep ahead of him, almost wrecking my car when I finally did find a place wide enough to pull over. Maybe he was having a problem with his brakes and couldn't gear down. Or maybe up until then it had just been a dull day.

Something just seems to happen to people in cars. Normally timid souls too afraid to bruise a tomato turn into animals behind the steering wheel. It must be the sense of security that being behind closed doors in their own

powerful machine somehow gives to them. They dart in and out of traffic, gesture obscenely with their fingers and yell profanities in the safety of deafening traffic noises.

Its possible, of course, that I am exaggerating and my years in traffic simply have taken their toll on my own nerves. Maybe that's why I can relate to the miserable soul out on Dixie Highway, as reported by Louisville newspapers, who had a skin full too. It seems that he was stalled in traffic, his car wouldn't restart and an anxious motorist behind him kept honking his horn.

The stalled driver, hot and frustrated, went back to discourage the horn blowing only to find that the driver, sensing some risk, had quickly rolled up his windows and locked his doors.

They say that by the time the police came to take the stalled car's driver away, the car behind him had stopped honking but was easily identified by the boot prints on its hood and roof.

The newspapers never reported what happened to either participant, but someone should have given one of them a medal. He left behind, I am sure, one more timid soul who is now the same way behind the wheel.

I've often felt like doing something like that myself but didn't have the guts. Besides, violence will never solve traffic problems. But, I do admit to feeling little sympathy for anyone who sits behind a hopelessly stalled car, blowing their horn, when helping to get the car started, or simply going around, would seem to be a much better solution. There's fewer boot prints that way.

After seeing how many people ignore emergency vehicles, run red lights, and zoom around me to beat me to the next traffic jam, I have little hope that conditions will ever improve. Maybe more sensitivity training, along with better drivers ed, would help. But, I don't think so.

On the other hand, I bet that I will get a good trade-in allowance for my low mileage, garage kept old car if, and when, I ever decide that I need a new one.

ON HIGHER EDUCATION

Several years ago, when I was first introduced to the business world, it became apparent rather quickly that people with college educations were observed differently from those without a degree. It was not that they were necessarily more successful or brighter or more capable - they were just observed differently. If two people of equal capabilities were competing for the same position, the nod usually went to the college graduate because he or she was perceived to be more rounded and had demonstrated that extra measure of personal achievement.

People like me, with only a high school education, had to work harder to succeed, relying on experience, native intelligence and common sense.

And then as it sometimes happens, when our extra effort and experience placed us in an advantaged position, we could be real smug in our conversations with college graduates. "I ain't got much formal education," we'd say, "but I do have common sense."

That's so they'd know the difference between them and us.

But then, after several years of extra effort and experience had paved the way to at least modest success, my native intelligence generated an amazingly brilliant thought. What if someone who had this abundant common sense could couple it with a college degree? That person should really have an edge, wouldn't he?

So I worked hard; went to night school; gave up television and ball games with the kids; listened to what a waste of time it was from neighbors who thought I should be mowing grass; and, finally, after five years or so, had a degree.

Then an even more brilliant thought occurred, already demonstrating the value of my new combination of formal education and common sense. If one degree was good, two should be stupendous. (By this time, a few big words had begun to work their way into my previously sparse vocabulary.) Maybe I could even add a professional designation as well so that someday I could stretch out those initials behind my name the way college professors like to do, when they write their credentials up on the blackboard at the beginning of a new class.

So I went back to school and put in another three years of hard work missing ball games, etc. and earned an M.B.A. And that, in turn, helped me get an interview with a public accounting firm that offered me a job at a twenty-five per cent cut in pay. Already anyone who knew me could see that my common sense was beginning to dim - I took the job.

Now it gets even more confusing. My level of success has been even greater than I ever expected but I still run into people from time to time who are far more successful - and without the benefit of a college education. When we talk about their careers, something has a familiar ring.

"I ain't got much formal education," they say, "but I do have common sense."

That's so I'll know the difference between me and them.

Life gets curious, don't it?

ON DOCTORS

In 1984 my wife almost died. Early in the year she developed a strange combination of seemingly unrelated illnesses that started with a severe pain shooting through her right arm and later localizing in her legs. At the same time, she had frequent problems with eating, low blood pressure, loss of stamina and other milder conditions. She became progressively worse with long periods of weight loss broken by brief periods of improvement in appetite, but always with the constant pain in her legs, from the groin to the knees. We grew concerned to the point of changing from the respected family doctor to a respected group of doctors. None could find a cause.

They ran extensive tests, called in specialists, performed a hysterectomy and did all the things they honestly thought needed to be done. But the pain and weight loss persisted and, now worse, she had great difficultly recovering from the operation and had to be taken back to the hospital or doctors frequently for intravenous liquids to prevent dehydration and to stabilize the low blood pressure.

In short, she was dying and no one knew from what.

One of the doctors, apparently a spokesman for the majority of the partners, told her they could not find anything wrong with her and the illness had to be psychological. Translation: If I don't see it, it ain't there.

By this time, Elizabeth was too sick and weak to risk the long trip to Mayo's or one of the better-known clinics but neither she nor I were ready to give up. We learned that the nearby University of Louisville School of Medicine sometimes conducted clinics on hard-to-solve cases. Through one of her doctors, through another doctor, we were able to get her an interview with the medical school's Chief of Staff, Dr. Hiram Polk. We had no idea at the time of the stature Dr. Polk held in the international medical community but from our brief interview we could tell we were in good hands

Dr. Polk seemed intrigued by the several serious but seemingly unrelated symptoms. He had been given Elizabeth's complete medical history along with the results of all the tests, X-Rays and related examinations over the past nine months or so and found the efforts to have been extensive, but not exhaustive.

He was also familiar with the reputation and credentials of the eight or nine doctors who had participated and respected their competence as physicians and surgeons. So did we.

The problem was whether Elizabeth's illness was physical or mental. And if it was physical, what was it? Dr. Polk concluded from his interview and examination that it had to be physical but agreed to conduct the clinic if Elizabeth would also submit to a psychiatric examination during her hospitalization. He arranged for her admission three weeks later that coincided with his return from a teaching engagement in China.

Elizabeth was met at the hospital by an intern who examined her case history and from there a procession of interns and assistants compiled test data and information for five of the most prominent specialists in Louisville. They, in turn, examined and reported as a week of testing passed. The psychiatrist gave her a clean bill of health.

At the beginning of the second week, however, Dr. Polk's assistant reported to us that Dr. Polk was out of town overnight but that the other doctors had met and felt that whatever the problem was, it was no longer there. The point of attack would now be therapy and nutrition. Translation: If I don't see it, it ain't there.

Before the new approach could develop, Dr. Polk returned and, apparently, did not agree with the conclusion. He replaced the internist with another who was also an endocrinologist. Within three days, Elizabeth's condition was diagnosed and temporary medication prescribed while further tests were being conducted to locate the source of her problem.

It turned out to be a failure of the pituitary gland to stimulate the adrenal gland that produces an essential body chemical. The diagnosis: Addison's Disease.

Elizabeth told me she could literally feel the pain leaving her legs as the medication was being administered. The next day her appetite and ability to hold down food began to improve. By the eighteenth day, when all tests were completed and we left the hospital, she was well on her way to full recovery.

We still don't know why it was so difficult to diagnose Elizabeth's condition. We understand that Addison's Disease had been around for a long time although it seems to affect different people in different ways. There was no known treatment until the early seventies and we are grateful there is one now.

What we do know is that Elizabeth was dying, literally in the arms of a battery of extremely competent and respected medical professionals who-- except for Dr. Polk, the psychiatrist and one or two others-- thought her problems were all mental.

That's where I have my problem. In my own case, I carried the professional designation of Certified Public Accountant. Although I was only in public practice for a short period of time, I know that there are thousands of CPA's out there who know more than I do; but none of them know it all. They simply can't; the field is too complicated. Yet, I wonder how many who practice in the profession simply give up on a problem or render inadequate opinions because of their limited knowledge or professional pride.

Of course, CPA's deal only with the financial well-being of an individual and while that is important, it is rarely a life-threatening situation.

Our doctors went farther than that. But what happens to all of those other people out there like Elizabeth in the hands of well-intentioned and, yes, competent doctors whose condition slips through a limited field of knowledge, and who do not have the resources to persist, or the good fortune to stumble upon a Dr. Polk?

The critical path from sickness to recovery took Elizabeth to many decision points over a full year of steadily diminishing health. As the pain persisted and her body became a shadow of her original self, there were numerous opportunities to give up--blamelessly. Yet, today, she is leading a full, normal life.

Dr. Polk, in his initial interview, described another woman who also had unusual symptoms and who had been diagnosed as mentally ill because the doctors could not find a physical source for her problem. "She was crazy when she came here," he said, "but once we found her problem and it was corrected, she wasn't crazy anymore." He was not belittling anyone's efforts but stating the truth that an undiagnosed physical problem can cause mental anguish to the point of incompetence, which may then become the problem itself in the eyes and minds of the medical professional.

But don't misunderstand me. I respect doctors greatly. My only daughter is a doctor. It is just that we perceive doctors as being somewhat above mere mortals when they hold life or death in their hands. We place our full faith in them and often look for miracles. The disappointment comes when we finally realize that they, too, are only human.

Dr. Polk made us no promises except an exhaustive effort to the level of local expertise to find the problem. He also acknowledged that their level of knowledge was incomplete and even if they were unable to determine the cause of Elizabeth's illness, some other clinic might.

He did not buy the crutch of a mental diagnosis and neither did he assume that there was no answer simply because some very fine doctors had failed to find it.

How fortunate for us that a man of his stature took that attitude. How unfortunate for others when their doctors do not.

ON SMALL TALK

One of my most prized possessions is the following letter I received several years ago.

Dear Gene,

I wanted to thank you for something you said in passing a number of years ago when you worked at McGrain & McCauley, CPA's.

We were all on break one day and were discussing going to school (college) as an adult. I had expressed an interest in returning to school but was reluctant at that time for a number of reasons. You said, "If you don't start now, by the time you are 35 you will be just where you are today.. . still thinking about it."

Well, I did return to school...and I am 35 years old...and last night I graduated from Indiana University Southeast.

I wanted to thank you for those words. I thought of them many times, particularly when things got a bit tough. Best wishes to you.

Sincerely

Jill

There is a great pride of achievement in that letter, rightfully deserved. Jill had a lot of things to straighten out in her life and she did. But the thought that a little break time conversation, small talk, could have that kind of impact on a person's life is a humbling feeling. And to think that letter would share an occasion as important as her graduation from college - after such a long and grueling sacrifice - with me the very next day still makes me feel both warm and frightened.

Obviously Jill wanted to go back to school and get her degree or she would not have done it. But perhaps she was on the brink of a decision that particular day and our seemingly innocent conversation provided the impetus for her to commit. Once the commitment was made the "I can do it" chant built inside her only to be silenced when the goal was reached. I did not deserve the credit she gave me but I will always be grateful for the acknowledgment.

I also received a similar letter years ago that I wish I had kept. In it the young lady informed me that she was leaving our company, with regrets, to help her husband in his growing and successful business. She had been with the company for some twelve years and I had forgotten about her in my several moves around the country. But when I received her letter I remembered Eula Mae. She was just out of high school, unpolished and plain, but with a solid academic background. She was backward and shy, applying for a job that required customer contact and I had grave doubts about hiring her. But something about her said she needed that job desperately. I gave her the opportunity and I was never disappointed. What Eula Mae lacked in personality and polish, she made up for in dedication and perseverance. Then she matured in a year or two, like a butterfly emerging from a cocoon, into the ideal person for the job. Bright, alert, attractive, personable and, yes, still dedicated.

Eula Mae acknowledged her gratitude to me for having given her a chance to prove herself when so many others had not. I had forgotten; she had not.

More recently I had the occasion to hire a new secretary and among the candidates was another Eula Mae, with sound credentials but lacking in confidence and social skills. She, too, had already been turned down for a number of secretarial jobs. I was discussing the similarities with my wife one evening after she had inquired how the search was going. Small talk. But this job was even more

important than the one Eula Mae did for me and I, again, had grave doubts. Then a voice came from the next room that helped me make the decision. It was my young daughter who I didn't even know was listening. She said: "Give her the job, Daddy."

I did, and although circumstances allowed her to work for me only a short time, I have observed her progress ever since. She did turn out to be another Eula Mae, growing in confidence and blossoming into an attractive, efficient secretary who would be welcome in any organization.

There have been other examples of the fine line that separates personal opportunity and growth from obscurity and failure in other people's lives that I have seen over the years. And I have received other letters acknowledging my inspiration or influence upon their lives.

I am proud of the ones I was able to help; disappointed in the ones where things didn't quite turn out the way either one of us had hoped. But the gnawing thought that hangs with me is the impact that some innocent word, some fateful decision, can have on the lives of others.

Some, like Eula Mae, we can observe. Others, like Jill, we only know about if they tell us. Yet, we keep talking, and we are comforted by the lack of awareness of what our words may mean to someone else.

That's good. It would be too much of a burden to dwell upon whose life we are touching today. Especially with small talk.

If we thought about it very much it could easily make stammering idiots of us all.

ON DISCIPLINE

Someone I know and truly respect always was generous to a fault to his employees, coddling and encouraging them until something happened which cost them his favor. Usually, I suspect, it resulted from them reading more into the relationship than he did. When they stopped earning, and started expecting, favored treatment, he could cut the cord very quickly. And when he was through, he was through, leaving the individual wondering what he or she had done wrong. He would never acknowledge these situations existed but, indirectly, he explained it all to me one day in a single philosophical gem: "I like to spoil people, but I hate spoiled people."

Getting that proper balance between encouragement and discipline is one of our greatest challenges, whether its dealing with employees, raising children or anything else involving human relations. It is in the giving and the taking, that delicate midpoint where the reasonable expectations of both parties meet, that the rewards are highest. Discipline, administered with self-discipline, should be the guiding principle.

My best example of this came to me from a most unlikely source. It involves my son, then five or six, who, along with two of his friends, had been pestering some older kids playing kick ball in the street. Although the older boys were only seven or eight themselves, Charlie and his friends were considered too young to join in the game. The younger boys responded by sitting in the grass with a handful of gravel that they would toss out into the street periodically to annoy and distract the older boys.

I learned of all this when I answered the front door to find Charlie standing wide-eyed and visibly shaken before me; held erect by a red headed, freckled representative of the kick ball team. The youngster, continuing to hold Charlie by the back of his shirt collar, explained to me what had happened and ended with such a positive and mature statement that I still cherish it to this day:

"I figured it was better to bring him home than to beat him up."

I agreed, both with concealed amusement and sincere praise to the young boy for having demonstrated such good judgment and self-discipline under the circumstances. Few adults would have handled it as well.

Wielding discipline with that same velvet touch should be a goal for every parent, employer and law enforcement officer. It represents correction without alienation and sets the examples that perpetuate sound teaching techniques of the behavioral patterns most of society prefers.

Sometimes, though, that learning experience becomes strained as any parent who has lived through their son or daughter's teenage years understands. The tension can lead to confrontation and the course that takes can affect the parent-child relationship, good or bad, for years to come. The balance is delicate and there is no computer model available that could predict the outcome. The variables in personalities, experience, physical characteristics and everything else are simply too indefinable. What takes over is a combination of experience, instinct and luck, the latter perhaps being the dominant force.

My most memorable, and only serious, confrontation with Charlie came when he was a junior in high school. With both of my children this seemed to be their most difficult year. They felt both the normal urges for the freedom of adulthood and the confining restrictions of parental and school authority. The life span behind them felt so brief, but the short year and a half to graduation and freedom seemed so distant and out of reach.

I don't remember what brought us to this particular confrontation but it became fairly serious and I sensed Charlie's anxieties and hostilities growing to the point where he was ready to reach out and strike someone, even me. I tried to exercise calmness and control as I invited him to do so. But with a few conditions.

I never recall ever wanting to hurt my own father, but I have seen that temptation in others many times. It seems to come during adolescence when a young man's growing sense of masculinity reaches the point where he suddenly feels big enough and strong enough to whip the old man; he doesn't have to take all his noise anymore. I told Charlie he certainly could take that chance if he ever felt that was something he really wanted to do. However, in this case the victor would get no spoils. When that day came, Charlie would have to be ready to leave - win, lose or draw - since both of us could not live in the same house anymore. But when he really felt that there was no other solution, when he absolutely had to vent his anger on some member of the family, and when he thought he could get the job done, all he had to do was let me know. We would take it outside and get it on.

Fortunately Charlie never took me up on that offer. And as he grew to his adult size of two hundred plus pounds wrapped athletically around a six-foot-three frame, there is no doubt in my mind that he could handle both me and that red haired, freckled faced boy from his childhood any day of the week. But that's not the message.

Charlie always was a good, decent boy who grew into a good, decent young man and, later on, a caring and responsible parent. I am very proud of his personal achievements and the character he has exemplified in all his scholastic, athletic and professional endeavors. Still we have friendly disagreements from time to time, but as any tension starts to build, Charlie grins at me and says, "Okay, old man, let's take it outside."

I sense from these times of good-natured confrontation that the more emotional one long ago had a lasting impact. In retrospect it was probably a stupid solution; and, I guess I was lucky it turned out the way it did.

Anyway, whenever he does extend the invitation to me these days, I am glad to see it worked. I've always been happy to see him smile.

ON NAIVETY

When I was very young, I was naive. Now, when I am much, much older, I still may be. My last psychological profile, taken a few years ago, says I never improved.

I graduated from high school in 1953 and immediately went to work for a factory up north. After a month of sleepless days, each followed by trying to work at night, I quit and joined the army. When I got out of the army, jobs were scarce and I went to work for a finance company.

All of this time I had been exposed to authoritarian figures; my father, my teachers, my foreman, my drill sergeants and my commanding officers. It is little wonder that as I entered civilian life, I accepted without question or reservation, the rules of my employment. The one about non-fraternization with employees kept me from accepting a date with a co-worker to whom I was genuinely attracted.

In my years with the finance company, I did what I was expected to do. If the situations called for walking five miles up a remote hollow of the Eastern Kentucky mountains, I did it. They were paying me for my results and, as I was often reminded, God didn't put a meter on my hips.

I did the work blindly. Once, to collect a thirteen-dollar balance, I walked three miles in snow almost knee deep only to find the debtor not at home. I tracked him all the way across the county until I found him and collected what he owed us. It wasn't the amount; it was the principle of the thing. If they owed, they paid. My supervisor was delighted.

Another time, following a major flood, I hand walked a wire cable, which used to be a swinging bridge, just to get to a customer who was past due only because he couldn't get across the river. He paid me the payment and then he, his family and some of their neighbors came down to the river to see me hand walk the cable back across.

Why did I do that? Why did I press perfectly cooperative and honest people to suffer financial sacrifices to repay loans provided at what some considered exorbitant interest rates to owners who eventually left millions to their wives? Wives - who, in turn - gave much of their fortunes to their favorite charities and universities. Would it not have been better, and more efficient, to let some of those poor loan customers keep their money to feed and school their own children and let some of those college students pay for their own education?

It was not my responsibility to judge; only to collect. And I did it efficiently, not with strong-arm tactics, but with the techniques of a salesman, that led to promotions so I could teach others how to collect with the same efficiency. And so that the owners of the company could elevate their lifestyle beyond imagination at the expense of many honest, hardworking disadvantaged people who often could not afford to repay their debts.

We provided a needed service in the aggregate; but, at my level we didn't deal with "aggregates," we dealt with individuals. That's why there were times that my conscience really suffered, as much as I believed that what I was doing was right. The people owed an honest debt; they ought to pay it. But I know for a fact that the repayment of a debt cost one woman her milk cow; it cost another man shoes for his children the next school year. Looking back, none of us could ever be proud of that. Nothing spoils a memory like the truth.

One of our techniques was to renegotiate a loan wherein the debtor obtained a qualified person to assure the payment of his debt. The approach was psychological and very successful. One of my co-workers described it as "conspiring with a deadbeat to defraud an honest man." Somehow, that summed it up. That practice, fortunately, was abandoned many years ago.

My only excuse for those earlier years is that I was young and naive. I believed what my superiors were telling me. I could only imagine the wild financial success that my efforts helped bring to the owners of the company. And maybe that was the problem. I was conditioned to believe that if I worked hard enough, and did what I was told to do, someday I might have those same things for myself.

Even now, when I see things happen which promote the interests of certain people over others, I can rationalize the outcome. That's what free enterprise is all about. If it fails, we all lose. If it's successful, we all win.

That's why it pays to keep a little naivety in your back pocket. It helps you stay in the game.

If a person becomes too cynical chasing the American dream, he may end up losing his turn. We've all worked too hard, made too many sacrifices, to have that happen to us.

ON GOOD OLD BOYS

You say you don't know what a "good old boy" really is. I don't know exactly what one is either. But from my mountain background and southern exposure, I have a pretty good idea. In fact, I think I grew up in the shadow of one - my brother, Darrell. What makes me think so is that on one of my visits back to West Virginia several years ago, I was pulled over at night on a long, dark stretch of country road by a deputy sheriff. Since I had out-of-state plates on my car, that part probably wasn't unusual. The thing that was is that he looked at my driver's license, then looked at me and asked: "Are you Darrell's brother?" My stomach tightened a bit as I admitted that I was. A big smile broke out across the deputy's face. "How the hell is old Darrell?" he asked, as my stomach tension began to release.

He spent the next few minutes reliving several of the good times that he and many others had had in the company of "Old Darrell" at Ma's Hut and Jimmy's Tavern. Darrell was a talented artist, poet and storyteller who would regale his audience for hours for nothing but an occasional hamburger and a few beers. When he was home, that is. Darrell was not only a free spirit, but a restless one. He never stayed in any one place very long, but he left a string of good memories wherever he seemed to go.

By the way, I think the deputy forgot why he stopped me in the first place. We both just went on our separate ways, no doubt thinking about Darrell.

I have had the good fortune to have met and known several good old boys in my lifetime. Some were hardworking and some less ambitious. All seemed to enjoy good company and, occasionally, a few beers.

I think most people who are considered "good old boys" by outsiders get a bum rap. Too often, the term is used to describe mindless, shiftless ne'er-do-wells who drink too much and contribute little of a positive nature to society. Not so. Most of those I have known held steady jobs and only drank as long as their paycheck lasted. But I'm not trying to balance any kind of ledger; I just want to tell you about a few of the ones I've seen along the way and who, to me, were worth remembering.

First there was Tommy, a boyhood friend of mine. Tommy was stopped downtown one night by the local constable who only wanted to see him safely home. Tommy wouldn't hear of it. "You've got me dead to rights. I don't have no license plates on the car, my brakes don't work and there's a gallon of moonshine in the trunk." Tommy insisted that he be taken to jail.

Jail, in our scrap of West Virginia landscape, was only a holding cell in the small Town Hall; the actual jail was at the county seat across the mountain, a good half-hour away in one direction. There were only two people on duty and both of them knew and liked Tommy. If anything, they just wanted to hold him overnight. Tommy wouldn't hear of it. He was absolutely humiliated by the fact that they would even consider putting a hardened criminal like himself in that dinky little old holding cell. He demanded that the constables take him to the "real" jail at the county seat.

As the two constables were trying to decide what they were going to do, they looked around to see Tommy headed for the door. "Where're you going?" they yelled.

"I don't know about you guys," Tommy said, "but I'm going to go get me another beer."

Then there was Howard. He managed one of our offices in western Virginia and when Howard had a chance to come down out of the mountains to attend a manager's meeting in a big city like Louisville, Kentucky, he liked to let off a little steam. He was also a great storyteller so it was usually pretty crowded at his table. Some of us, originally from his neck of the woods, always liked to join him to swap a few stories.

At one of those meetings, we had our first woman in attendance, a sophisticated cashier supervisor just hired by the company and totally unfamiliar with mountain humor. She favored us with a visit to our table while she was working the room. I think Howard became a little inhibited by her presence because it wasn't too long until he excused himself to go to the restroom. In a few minutes, he staggered back out looking somewhat addled and rubbing his head. Our concerned cashier supervisor asked him what was wrong.

"I don't know," Howard replied. "I just knelt down at that spring in there to get me a drink of water and something fell down and hit me on the head."

The rest of the evening was spent without the pleasure of female companionship.

Cliff, another employee, only considered himself a social drinker but he almost always was sociable. However, one night at a company outing at the racetrack he did get a little rowdy. We had a rule that if anyone started getting out of line, one or two of his friends were given the responsibility of taking him back to the hotel and putting him to bed. The two assigned to Cliff decided, instead, to just take him out to the parking lot and let him sleep it off in the back seat of the car. They were still sitting in the front seat, talking, when Cliff awakened, rose out of the back seat, looked around the parking lot and tried to open the door. "Where're you going?" one of them asked.

"This damn traffic ain't going nowhere" Cliff replied. "I'm going to get out and walk."

Sometimes those good old boys didn't even belong to us. Like one time several of us had gathered in somebody's motel room playing guitars and banjos and singing country songs. The door was open and one of the other motel guests, who had a noticeable head start at the bar, ambled by.

"I heard your music," he said "and thought I'd stop by if you guys don't mind. My room is just across the hall."

We assured him we didn't mind but expressed our concern as to whether or not we were bothering him.

"Heck no!" he said. "I'm not even there."

Say you still don't know what a "good old boy" is. That's okay. Most of them wouldn't have enough room at their booth or table for an outsider anyway. But if you did stop by, they would treat you politely if you acted politely and friendly yourself. Being uppity won't cut it; buying the next pitcher of beer usually helps.

For my own part, the time I have spent in the company of good old boys has been highly enjoyable and has produced some of my fondest memories. But you know how it is. Good times can fog the senses. I can't be expected to remember them all.

ON RELIGION

I believe in God. But He already knows that. In fact, He and I had a very serious talk back in 1984 when Elizabeth was literally dying and I was helpless, by myself, to save her life. I asked for His help and her life was spared. That's how I know He is there for all of us who sincerely believe in Him. But I don't wear my religion on my sleeve. So if my beliefs don't conform to all of your beliefs, don't throw around words like atheist or agnostic. God knows better. I simply communicate with Him in my own way and it doesn't seem to bother Him at all.

I don't have any secrets from God - How could I? - and, as far as I know, He doesn't keep any from me. At least, none that I need to know. All He wants me to do is be as good a person as I can be and to respect His rules of right and wrong. That's why I feel no compulsion to attend any particular church on a regular basis. The modern ceremonies, robes and rituals make me feel uncomfortable. Of course, one might say that you're not supposed to feel comfortable attending church if you're still a sinner. Good point. Maybe some day, if that's what He wants me to do, I'll start attending regularly again. I'll just wait for Him to tell me which one.

Other people I know do associate their religion with a particular church, mosque or synagogue and, for them, I guess that's the right thing to do. It has always been confusing to me, though, that one God could have so many churches of so many different beliefs, with each proclaiming to be the only path to heaven. If that's true, most of us are in deep trouble just by the affiliation we've chosen.

I grew up with a strong church affiliation, starting it all with a performance of the infant Jesus in a pageant that made my parents proud. My Dad's favorite diversion was playing the organ and singing all the old gospel hymns. When I was a kid, I knew them all. The Regular Baptist Church was our family's chosen path to religion and we attended service practically every Sunday, some of the time walking a mile to get there. My father's influence even grew to the point that he was able to persuade the congregation to invite Brother Calvin to come over from his own church a couple of counties away to preach at a three week revival. Dad had gone to his church several years before and assured everyone that there was no other preacher like him in the world.

Brother Calvin agreed to come and everybody was impressed with the choice. Me too. He was just about the smoothest talking person I'd ever seen and a handsome man to boot. They put him up at the local hotel, with free room and board. On Sunday, he visited selected homes of church members, favoring one of them by staying for Sunday dinner. It was a real treat to have him come around.

But sometime before the revival was over Brother Cal took off, with all the money he had collected and the daughter of the man who owned the hotel. Keep in mind that this was long before television; when certain celebrated evangelists turned this type of religious deception into an art form. They would have been impressed. Brother Cal did it right.

I never knew what ever happened to him, or the money or the girl or his wife and family that he left behind. Dad didn't seem to want to talk about it much. But that never shook my faith in God; although I'll admit that my faith in some of His self-proclaimed messengers is still a little shaky.

My faith in God was strengthened even more after I met my father-in-law, Johnny Justice. Johnny belonged to a branch of the Baptist Church called Primitive Baptists. I have since learned that all churches calling themselves

51

Primitive Baptists are not the same but I like the one Johnny belonged to. It was a small church, tightly knit, and they took their religion seriously.

That's not to say that they were stuffed shirts about drinking or cussing or anything a man wanted to do. Far from it. What they believed was that a man made his own heaven or hell here on earth; and, there were no life hereafter or last minute confessions to bail him out. So if a man wanted to drink, let him drink. If God didn't like it, He'd let him know.

Another thing I liked about Johnny's church was that they didn't take up offerings, they didn't have an organist and they didn't pay the preacher. If the preacher had the calling, he had the calling. If the church needed fixing, they'd fix it. If somebody needed help, they'd help them. It was as simple as that.

But the absence in their religion of a heaven or a hell didn't mean they suspended honor for the dead. Every year the church held a memorial at the cemetery, a reunion of sorts, and it was all to remember those who had gone before. That was the only life after death they recognized, the continuation of life in the memory of those left behind.

Johnny was one of the best men I have ever known. He wasn't lily white; but he grew up and lived his life in a mountain culture where people were: good or bad, right or wrong, and the favorite quotation from the scriptures was "an eye for an eye". He lived every day as an honest, caring man who would literally give you the shirt off his back if you needed it. If you were just lazy, a liar or a cheat, Johnny had no use for you at all. He didn't try to "redeem" anyone; that was a personal choice. And he was a quiet man, short of stature but a man who could stand very tall in the defense of what he thought was right. He rarely volunteered his opinion about religion or anything else; but, if you really felt like you wanted it, Johnny was never hard to find.

That's what bothers me the most about the focus so many people place upon a particular religion or church instead of just making things right with God. I gave my children the same opportunity that I had to learn about the scriptures, about God, His various churches and the needs of the less fortunate around them. And they both still attend church regularly, each in his and her chosen faith. But, for me, it seems that a lot of churches today are more concerned about survival than revival, where the aim is saving souls. From what I've seen, the time devoted to taking up the offering is about equal to the sermon. Somehow that makes Johnny's beliefs just a little more believable every day.

Anyway, I do believe in life after death or at least that the spirit outlives the body. I've had that type of personal experience myself. I don't know how long it lasts or what it is really like since my own encounter was so brief. But I do know one thing. If there is life after death and good people like Johnny didn't make it into heaven, how in the hell am I going to?

And if he's not there, I'm not sure I want to go.

ON POLITICS

I think I've heard most of the reasons why people want to get into politics. They all have been pretty high sounding and convincing; passionate and persuasive to the person. A few of them could even shake their finger in your face and tell you the biggest lie you ever heard with the passion of a gospel evangelist. It makes great theater but falls a little shy of my idea of good government. Anyone who has noticed the scheming and maneuverings of some of our political bodies may be tempted to agree. A man of my own personal convictions would have to be a glutton for punishment, or indeed have a calling, to join that group only for the good of the people. But someone has to do it and I'm glad it's not me.

I held a statewide political appointment once, which I was talked into accepting against my better judgment and personal choice. It was supposed to have been as non-political as a political appointment could be, with all members working for the good of the state's entire population. Didn't work that way.

All politics require compromise and there are things better left to those who don't mind modifying a few principles or shading their ethics just a little bit. Situational ethics, I think they call it. I couldn't handle that part.

However, I do vote in every election and I vote for whomever I believe will do the best job, regardless of their motivation or their affiliation with one party or another. If I don't know a candidate well enough to make a choice, or if it doesn't make a difference to me, I don't vote for that particular office.

And match-book covers and pencils, handed out by the poll workers as you walk the gauntlet to the polling place--especially after you've parked four blocks away because all of the politicians and their workers have taken up all the nearby parking spaces--have yet to influence my decision. But maybe that comes from a personal observation I made several years ago.

My father-in-law worked hard for his party up in Eastern Kentucky. It was his job to help get out the vote by hauling people without a ride back and forth from home to the polling place. As was the custom in that time and place, he was usually assigned certain people and given a few half-pints and five-dollar bills to help keep the party faithful.

One election eve, he and his friend, Bill, were discussing how corrupt and undependable the voters had become in recent years.

"It's downright terrible," Bill complained. "Last time they'd take your whiskey and your money and go right inside and vote ag'in you. It's getting so you can't even buy an honest vote."

You never could fool those people in Eastern Kentucky either.

ON SEX

My first encounter with sex was too embarrassing to talk about so I'll go on to the second. That was Bernice.

Bernice was just coming into early womanhood and was also developing into a real tease. But the only thing she seemed to like about me was my red plaid shirt. One day I offered it to her but she wasn't interested. Then, later in the day when I came back from the store with some red cherry candy in my pocket, she changed her mind. It could have been the candy that did it; it was the round ball kind with a hard outer shell and a soft center. Candy can be a lot like people sometimes.

Anyway, once we were past the negotiating stage, we went up in the smoke house on the sawdust floor with Bernice there eating her cherry candy and me anxious to explore the mysteries of emerging womanhood. But somewhere in the process, her mother got worried about us and we both had to scramble to save our hides.

We explained that I was sharing my cherry candy with Bernice and we were hiding to keep my cousins from horning in. Bernice's mother knew my cousins so she understood. She also thought it was very generous of me to give Bernice my red plaid shirt. I couldn't tell her mother, of course, but to tell you the truth, Bernice hadn't come anywhere close to earning it yet.

My next experience was with an older girl who was visiting her aunt and uncle who were neighbors of ours. I had heard she had been in all kinds of trouble and that's why she was there staying for a while.

One night we were outside in the orchard while her aunt and uncle were visiting inside the house. At first it was just ordinary talk, but she kept leading the conversation into the kind of stuff that made me nervous with an older girl. Then she started making suggestive movements with her hands and asking did I know what this was or what that was.

Finally, I told her to wait a minute. I went in the house and told my older brother what she was doing. My brother was reading a book and he just got up, put down the book without even marking the page, and went outside. I don't know what happened after that but he sure was nice to me the rest of the time he was home.

I've learned a lot about sex since then and yet, even as I grow older, I'm never sure how much I've missed. Take the time in Paris when my friend, Tommy, and me, on the advice of a Belgian soldier we knew, went to the Ritz Hotel. Jean, the Belgian, had worked his way through Sorbonne University by entertaining middle aged women he met at the Ritz. They were usually wealthy widows or divorcees traveling through Europe who could be very generous to a young man who showed them some attention. Tommy and I took seats at the bar and looked around. There were several unescorted women there and they did look rich--but they also looked very old. When the bartender came over and asked us what we'd have, we looked around again, looked at each other and said, "nothing!" We left.

Since then, of course, the range of suitable ages has broadened greatly.

Over the years I've seen some men who made sex an art. And since I've already mentioned their names, both Tommy and Jean fit that mold. It was an education to see either of them at work, especially Jean, who had both the appearance and the suave mannerisms of the French actor, Charles Boyer. Tommy, on the other hand, was the baby-faced, kewpie doll type that women just seemed to want to cuddle.

One night in Barcelona he said he cuddled one twelve times. He had announced his intentions the evening before. Then he was going to raise the window, beat on his chest and yell like Tarzan. I never did hear any yell; but the next morning he said he just couldn't get the window up. All the senorita would say was that he was "mucho, mucho man!" Maybe the window really was stuck.

Even as educational as all this may be, some might say it tracks a little to the seamier side. Sex is really a beautiful experience and while love helps, it obviously isn't essential. Certain people are simply physically attracted to each other and when the chemistry is there, it's great. When it isn't, the words of an old country song remind us, "No it's not love, but it's not bad."

A friend of mine once summed it up in a way, whether original or not, which also expresses my own sentiments. He said he had never seen an ugly woman. I can't say I agree a whole one hundred percent with that particular observation, but I'm with him most of the time.

Especially when he said, "The worst I ever had was wonderful!"

There's a man who knew a thing or two about sex.

ON KEEPSAKES

When I was growing up, my father kept a metal box under his bed that we were never allowed to touch. Whatever was in it was personal and private and I always wondered what mysteries or treasures it held. Years later, after his death, its contents came to me in an envelope from one of my step mother's daughters who also sent me his old .12 gauge shotgun. She knew I wanted the gun for a special reason.

The envelope contained a few old letters and documents and a handful of keepsakes. Among them was the Purple Heart awarded posthumously to my brother, Paul, whose plane was shot down over the Pacific Ocean during World War II. There was also a medal Dad had won as runner-up in the West Virginia wood chopping championship back in the thirties; a report card of mine from a school year in which I had made straight A's; and, a few other items of recognizable memorabilia.

The most intriguing of all to me, though, was a thimble. It may have been my mother's or my grandmother's, but I don't really know. I only know that, for whatever reason, it was important to him and that its memories must have been much larger than the small finger it fit. Otherwise, it would not have deserved a place in that private metal box.

In my own jewelry tray is a set of cuff links made of ivory, or something

simulating ivory, mounted in 14-karat gold. I bought them in France nearly fifty years ago when I was in the Army. We were stationed at Fontainebleau, near Paris, and three of my buddies and I had two-year tours to serve overseas. One of the first things we did was scrape up $100 each and put it together to buy a 1947 Dodge Deluxe sedan from a sergeant who was returning to the states.

The car became more than a passport to the wonders of Europe; it made the four of us inseparable, closer than brothers, whose mobility was interdependent in a youthful world where each adventure was brand new.

Our next major investment was in a wardrobe worthy of our automobile, the first any of us had ever owned. Mine, acquired over time, consisted of a navy blue suit, a gray flannel suit and a powder blue flannel sport coat, all tailored by Alexander's of

England. Each outfit cost more than a month's pay and was set off by white-on-white shirts with French cuffs and Bostonian Prep wing tipped shoes. The gray flannel was the first new suit of clothes I ever owned.

We were a handsome, dashing group and the mobility afforded by our car took us from the canal streets of Amsterdam to the gypsy caves of Granada. We saw all the sights we wanted to see and did all the things we wanted to do, limited only by the collective funds we could save between trips.

When money was tight, we could dress up and go downtown to a little bistro where the equivalent of thirty cents would buy a loaf of French bread and a bottle of Beaujolais. The bread retarded the effects of the wine and you could literally spend a full evening with an empty billfold.

I still wear my ivory cuff links from time to time. Unlike the suits, the shoes and the shirts, they did not wear out or grow tighter in the waistband. They just lay there among the other cuff links, totally inconspicuous, meaning nothing to anyone except me. But when I put them on, I am tied to my youth, to a time of excitement and adventure, when the painted dancers at the Moulin Rouge would descend in their gilded cages to my feet and when the Champs Elysees and Rue Pigalle were as familiar to me as the only street in my hometown. They recall the faces and the names of my friends, like brothers no more, who surely have their own mementos and memories of those happy, fleeting years.

I have kept some of my father's keepsakes but their special memories are gone. The shotgun hung for years over my mantle until a house fire partially destroyed it but, although it was his gun, it was not his face I saw when I looked at it. It is Ethan's, my younger brother, who was perhaps ten or eleven years old that evening when Arch, one of the workers at the sawmill, came by the house after being out on a drinking spree.

Dad was gone and Ethan and I were home alone. Arch had gambling on his mind and insisted that I shoot dice with him, perhaps planning to win back some of the money he had spent on whiskey. I didn't want to play and told him I didn't have any money, but Arch was persistent, with emotions reaching hostility and intimidation.

He was a grown man with a large, but young, family and I was only in my early teens. I had no choice but to play and in the process, whether due to his intoxication or my own luck, I won what little money Arch had left.

He became angry and was at the point of attacking me when the nervous voice of my little brother came from the back of the room.

"You better not hurt my brother."

Ethan was standing there with Dad's loaded shotgun in his hands, aimed at both of us as directly as his frail and unsteady arms could manage and the look on his face left no doubt that he would pull the trigger.

I began to calm him down as Arch ran from the room and as soon as Arch was gone, Ethan let me take the gun. I never told Dad about that incident because of what he might have done to all of us. There is no doubt in my mind, though, that Ethan meant to protect me, at all cost, from the beating Arch was ready to give me--without realizing that I, too, was in his line of fire.

But what could have happened didn't. The memory, however, remains clear, in timeless recall, until the ruined remains of that old shotgun pass on to someone else.

That's how it is with keepsakes. The shotgun, the cuff links, an item here and there, are all silent reminders of special moments in my life. They will retain their form long after mine is gone. But they will never mean the same things to someone else that they mean to me. If they are kept by someone else after I am gone, it will be for someone else's reason, someone else's memory. No one but me can look at Dad's shotgun and see Ethan's face. No one but me can wear those cuff links and see the Eiffel Tower. And no one can touch that tarnished thimble and know the special meaning it held for my father years ago.

That's the good thing, and the bad thing, about keepsakes. They keep the heart warm and the memory alive but only for one person at a time. And they never yield their secrets, whatever they may be. Each person, if he chooses, gets to keep those for himself.

ON WINNING

She was six or seven; he was three or four. At the age when she was twice as fast and twice as smart, she had masterminded this footrace, set off the distance and made up the rules. Since she was a girl, she got a head start; since she was older, she would begin the count. Then, anticipating her own command, the "one, two, three, go!" had scarcely left her lips as she was crossing the finish line, breathless but delirious in her happiness; whereupon she probably voiced the understatement of her entire life:

"I like to win!"

I was amused as I watched my niece and nephew at play, realizing that she, in the honesty of youth, had expressed so openly the feelings she would always have, but learn to guard, as life placed the albatross of maturity around her neck.

For children, it is commendable to want to win; for adults, it is commendable to win, but never to give the hint that you want to. The idea is to learn to lose graciously, congratulate the winners on being the better team that day and to salvage victory from defeat with your demonstration of true sportsmanship.

That's probably the rationale used by whoever came up with the saying: It is not whether you win or lose, but how you play the game. Another like mind gave us: It is the thought, not the gift that counts. Both have a nice sound to them, but most of the people I know would grab for the win and the gift every time.

That's not to say that sportsmanship isn't an honorable and desirable trait. The very presence of competition assures that there will be winners and losers. It is when an unfair advantage leads to an inequality among competitors, and the victor fails to feel the hollowness of his own victory when he knew that he had little to risk, that there should be shame.

One man I know, with children older than the slender young boy he engaged in a one-on-one game of basketball, literally fouled, manhandled and battered his way to victory against his reluctant competitor. He apparently needed to prove to himself that a full grown, middle-aged man could "whip" a frail, intimidated young boy on a basketball court. For some reason, his ego apparently needed this type of reassurance and one can only speculate as to how often this cancer of insecurity must be fed and at whose expense.

My own wife, one of the most sensitive and gentle people I know, could become a raving maniac at a Little League game when our son was participating in the sport. It became so bad, in fact, that I often sat on the opposite side of the stands so as to become as disassociated as possible from her verbal attacks on the umpire whenever Charlie or his team got an adverse call. Charlie, in his mother's mind, had an absolutely infallible sense of the strike zone. If he struck at a ball, it was a strike. If he didn't, it was a ball. To have some biased umpire standing behind the plate for the sole purpose of helping out an inept pitcher was a total disgrace.

I never personally competed in organized team sports but I have occasionally competed one-on-one. It has not always been on equal footing and I have usually known when I had, or did not have, the edge. My biggest problem, however, has been an innate compulsion to play by the rules.

This flaw was punctuated one time in karate when, as a purple belt, I was free fighting a visiting lower grade belt of another discipline. The contest was progressing routinely until he kicked my legs out from under me with a sweep kick, a violation of our club's non-contact rules, and left me with a broken wrist. There are forfeiture rules that can be invoked when such things happen; and, of course, the violator can be draped in the shame of "unsportsman-like conduct."

But this young man simply was driven by natural instinct. In his mind, I imagine, he was only pursuing that same satisfaction my young niece was able to experience those many years ago when she so enthusiastically admitted: "I like to win!"

To many people, the choice to win by whatever means is easy to justify. A person can be the one sweep kicking his way through life - and winning - or the one nursing the broken wrist. Rules only complicate things. Besides, who in the world would ever expect a serious competitor to fully observe the rules anyway? You just don't see it that much in everyday life. Not even on Sunday. Not even when there are umpires, referees and line judges on the field.

It's too hard to win that way.

ON CONVERTIBLES

The first car my Dad owned during my childhood was a convertible. Before I was born, he had owned several cars, big and fancy ones I was told, but that was before the Great Depression. He had been a successful businessman back then, buying and selling timber, lumber and various wood products for building and mining. For two years into what was supposed to be a minor recession, he kept his men on the job, giving them work and stockpiling inventory that couldn't be sold. By the time the true depth of the Depression became clear, it was too late to salvage anything. After his business failed, he went to work in the coalmines and, almost immediately, suffered a broken back in a slate fall. He regained much of his physical strength but he never recovered financially. I'm sure there also was a part of his spirit that was left behind in those decaying stacks of mining timbers and lost horizons.

After all those years of seeing Dad walk home from work at night, it was both a surprise and a pure delight when he drove home one day in a red and black 1929 Model A Ford roadster. Even though the car was fifteen years old or more, it was still a real beauty. The convertible top had roll up window flaps and there was a rumble seat in the back for my brother and me. He drove us in to town to try it out. We couldn't have been more proud if it had been a brand new Lincoln.

Practicality soon took over, however, and Dad removed the rumble seat, replacing it with a homemade truck bed so he could haul things in it and sell produce from it. In my young mind, that was a terrible thing to do to a fine looking car like ours.

My love affair with convertibles still remained strong and I always pictured myself grown up with an Errol Flynn mustache, behind the wheel of a bright red beauty with the top back and the wind caressing my hair as I cruised the highways of the world. Instead, my first car was a 1941 Plymouth with a damaged passenger side door that I bought in 1953 for $100. I had it less than one month before I joined the Army.

I was stationed in France for most of my Army tour and much of that time I shared ownership of an old sedan with three of my friends. But the place was full of those European roadsters and I wanted one so bad I could taste it. Especially the British MG - the one with the old body style that's such a classic today. They quit making that model in 1956, the year I was discharged. I could have brought a brand new one home for $1,600, duty free. The $75 a month I had saved for college would have paid for most of it, but I guess that practicality must be genetic. I waited until I got home and spent $225 for a 1949 Oldsmobile sedan instead.

Later that same year, I was visiting one of my sisters when my older brother, Darrell, came by. He was driving a spanking new 1956 Ford Victoria convertible. It was baby blue - with the top down, of course, so you could see the beautiful white leather interior. He and his wife talked me and my younger brother into taking a trip in it that very evening to see another sister who lived about 200 miles away.

Convertibles are pretty but I can tell you that riding in the back seat of one of those things for 100 miles or so over two lane roads, with dirt and bugs hitting you in the face, can kill a dream real quick. It was also cold in the back seat. Darrell was happy as a lark up front. Up there, the bugs hit the windshield instead of your face and the heater kept your legs and feet warm. He put up a spirited argument before we could talk him into pulling over and putting the top up. What's the use of having a convertible if you can't ride with the top down?

The following spring, Darrell still had the car and he insisted that I take my girlfriend out in it one Sunday. He lived where she did and I was working about 100 miles away. I still hadn't really experienced the full enjoyment of a convertible from the front seat so I took him up on the offer. I drove over Sunday morning and exchanged cars with him for the day. All in all, my girlfriend and I had a real good time driving around and visiting people in that beautiful, baby blue convertible while Darrell was doing whatever he was doing in my old Oldsmobile.

What he was doing, it turned out, was using up all my gasoline. I had a three-hour drive back over the mountains to my job so I returned his car by seven o'clock, ready to get on the road. Darrell didn't show up until after eleven. He didn't seem the least bit concerned that it would be two o'clock in the morning before I would get to bed; and, he also didn't bother to tell me about using all my gas. With no service stations open at that time of night, I ended up parking beside of one about half way home and spending the rest of the night in my car. When I got to work the next morning, I was not only late but noticeably haggard from the night before. My boss asked me what happened. I told him. He thought it was funny. I didn't.

As it turned out, I never did own a convertible. They even quit selling standard models in this part of the country for a long time. But now, even if I had one, I don't have that much hair left for the wind to caress and I still haven't developed an appetite for low flying bugs.

Still, every time I see one of those old classic MG's, I think about how close I came to owning one and what fun it would be to find one again. I have to wear glasses anyway, so maybe I could just get a pair that was slightly tinted, so I could still see but it wouldn't look like I really needed them. Then I could get me one of those little English golf caps to keep what's left of my curls in place. And if I could just learn to keep my mouth shut and breathe through my nose, the bugs may not be so bad. I might even benefit from the exercise, just trying to get in and out of one of those little things. Maybe I could even. . .

Nah.

ON CREATING WEALTH

When my daughter, Sharon, reached the point in her career where she could think about investing on a regular basis, she asked for my advice. This was a far cry from the situation several years ago when she returned from college with a medical degree in hand, along with two young children and four years of student loans to repay. She and her husband, a newly graduated Ph.D. himself, were house hunting with no income other than her expected stipend as an intern at University Hospital. I kept taking them to houses I thought they could barely afford even if both of them were working. It soon became evident that the houses that fit their pocketbook didn't quite fit their new image of themselves. I took them to breakfast to discuss the situation. After awhile, Sharon seemed to understand the position they were in. Her husband, however - remembering the struggle, I suppose, that both of them had endured while starting a family and completing some eight years of college - made his state of mind quite clear: "I'm tired of being poor."

As far as I know there are few known cures for that condition. None of them include going into debt deeper than you can afford.

They did, in fact, settle for a nice, but affordable, house at that time. However, extravagance later pushed them deeply in debt. Now divorced, Sharon is steadily moving toward financial independence.

When she sought my advice about investments, I gave her the usual do's and don'ts that a former banker and C.P.A. would normally offer. She wanted something more specific, like where and how to invest in the stock market. She already was buying her home and had paid off her car, furniture and credit cards - excellent first steps. She also had reasonable insurance coverage, including a fairly substantial term life policy. Now she wanted to develop a workable plan to secure her financial future.

What secures a person's financial future, of course, is a personal thing. Some people will have more modest needs or a lesser ability to accumulate wealth than others. But how much is enough? For my Dad, after years of financial struggle, it was twenty acres of hillside land. It had plenty of timber, water and enough bottomland to grow vegetables and livestock. And it also had its mineral rights intact. Dad said he owned that land from heaven to hell; and, as long as he did, "I don't have to beg nobody's pardon." Maybe that is the right goal; when a person accumulates enough wealth to feel financially secure and comfortable enough that he or she no longer feels the need to beg anybody's pardon.

What follows is not intended to be a tutorial on anything. It is simply a little advice, given to my daughter, who apparently senses - with some appreciation, I hope - that I am now able to enjoy the same mindset as my father.

Since I don't invest, personally, in real estate - I can't fix my own plumbing, much less answer some tenant's cry in the middle of the night - I have never pursued this popular avenue to riches. In fact, I tend to invest in only those things that do not require my personal participation in either a management or advisory capacity. That, principally, is the stock market.

-- The stock market is no place to put money that you may need in the near term: to pay taxes, meet emergencies and so forth. Instead, open an account with a broker recommended by someone you trust and who has successfully negotiated those troubled waters. The monthly statements from the brokerage firm will keep you informed of your progress or serve as a reminder that you are not following your plan conscientiously enough.

-- Build up the Money Market segment of that account until you feel comfortable enough to invest part of it in stocks. If you do not absolutely have to, do not use its check writing features for anything except investment or investment related taxes and expenses.

-- Unless you are willing to do research and monitor your stock portfolio, consider a mutual fund in an area you know something about. These are not my personal preference, since such funds charge management and administrative fees on a recurring basis as well as a commission, or load, which they often charge up front. This reduces the amount invested immediately. In addition, the larger a fund becomes, the more difficult it is for the fund manager to keep finding good quality stocks with the desired expected returns. This sometimes results in the fund being closed, then sold on the market like regular common or preferred stock. I like such "closed end" funds better since there is more predictability to the fund's composition and yield; and, purchase and sales transactions are cheaper and easier.

-- Look for stocks with strong name recognition and fundamentals, which are selling in the teens, twenties or thirties. Penny stocks sell for such prices for a reason and picking survivors is like drawing to an inside straight. Stocks selling above $40 seem to plummet much faster in a market downturn as investors try to salvage their portfolio or protect their gains. The stocks within the teens to thirties range tend to recover their losses more quickly, and provide a greater upside potential in percentage gains, when the market improves.

-- Set a price target and sell when the target is reached. If the target is to double, and that happens while the stock is still moving upward, a good alternative is to sell half the holdings, thereby recovering the full original investment. Now you are playing on the house's money on the half you kept. But watch it! It's still money and if you ever use "stop losses," use them now.

-- A Stop Loss order, in fact, is a good thing to have on all your stocks. It is an order to sell the issue if the stock drops to or below a certain price. Thus, while you may not maximize a profit, you can avoid severe losses - except when something happens so damaging to a stock that it slides so rapidly there simply is no market at the price in the order. Some people worry that a drop of ten or fifteen percent will only be temporary and they will not only sell out of a stock they wanted to keep, but also trigger those dreaded income taxes on any gain. In my opinion, keeping a declining stock simply to avoid paying taxes is foolhardy. Paying taxes means you are making money. I like to pay taxes.

-- Watch what is happening to your stocks. Since I am a subscriber to their Internet service, I use America On Line's market summary to keep track of what is happening to my stocks on a daily basis. It only takes a few minutes to read the price changes and the news. And if I don't keep up with them, who will?

-- Don't panic in down markets. If a slide in the market is causing mental anguish or loss of sleep, you have no business being in the market. But don't be foolish, either. If it looks like a stock you own is headed for the bottom, take your lumps and get out.

-- A depressed market can be a very good time to restructure your portfolio. Some good stocks will have dropped faster than others but are just as likely to recover. If one has held its value better, it may be worthwhile to sell it and buy more of the lower priced stock. In a market recovery, the upside potential and percentage return may be far greater.

-- Understand that stocks rise and fall, depending upon whether or not they are in favor with the investment community. Large investors - especially pension fund and mutual fund managers - who have been burned in a severe downturn are understandably cautious about putting sidelined money back into the market. Often the viability of a particular company may be serious; but, just as often, the turnaround situation investors are trying to predict may be of short term or moderate duration. Look at these stocks carefully. I still have Citigroup stock that I bought, under its original Citibank structure, for $9.00 per share, before splits. Even though it was the largest bank in the United States, many analysts were predicting eminent doom or a very long recovery period. Neither happened.

-- A Reverse Split in a stock is a bad sign, in my opinion, and screams out for the holder to sell. This sometimes happens when a company's stock has gone through a period of depressed market pricing to where it fears a de-listing with its exchange. A one-for-five or one-for-ten reverse stock split tends to present a more favorable market price when it first occurs, but it is still the same company. If you hang on to your now fewer shares of stock, be prepared to see them slide back down.

--Be wary of brokers' or analysts' advice. When you receive their list of recommended stock picks, read the footnotes. They often acknowledge that their firm makes a market in that stock or that they either have, or are currently, participating in other financial activities with the company they are recommending. Some investment advisory companies, such as Value Line, have no such ties to the companies included in their analytical research for which they charge a relatively high fee. So, some advice is free and some is expensive. But some "free" advice can be even more expensive.

--Bonds - treasury, treasury agencies, corporate and/or municipal - can be sound, meaningful additions to a quality investment portfolio in levels depending upon the investor's objectives, age and tolerance for risk. Bonds tend to be more predictable with respect to an income stream and safer with respect to return of capital. Steer clear of options, bond derivatives and other forms of investment alternatives you don't understand. It is better to have passed up a fortune than to lose one. The pain can last forever.

Of course there's more to creating wealth than this. The range of possibilities is much broader and I'm still learning myself. But I know that investing in the stock market can be a gamble. In the words of Kenny Rogers' famous song, "You've got to know when to hold them; know when to fold them; know when to walk away; and, know when to run." Getting out of a stock is just as important as getting in. No one can "time" the market. Just because a stock once sold for $90 and is now selling for $10 doesn't mean it is a bargain. And averaging down - buying the stock at its lower price to reduce your average cost from having bought it at the higher price - doesn't always mean you will recover anything.

Over the long haul, well-selected stocks tend to generate solid returns but patience is required. The quick big hits that some people realized during the initial surge of the technology era were fabulous when the investors got in and got out in time. So are the fortunes of those holding winning lottery tickets. Few estates are built that easily.

The creation of wealth for most people is a slow process and requires the development of a livable, workable plan. Once you have it in place, follow the plan. Add to the investment account regularly as though it is a bill you absolutely have to pay. Then, resist dipping into your growing asset to satisfy some unnecessary whim or desire. But, when you have accumulated enough to feel comfortable in your financial security, start spending some of it. If you don't, rest assured; your children will.

ON COPING

I don't know if anybody else has had this experience or not. You hear some statement or phrase that sticks with you throughout your life, popping up at the strangest times to provide guidance, comic relief or maybe for no apparent reason at all. I have several that give me my direction but the first one I remember may be this simple, innocuous experience that helped me to integrate those that would follow into my overall philosophy of life.

It came when my father, brother and I were visiting a neighbor back when I was a kid. The neighbor was plowing a field with a young horse he had recently acquired and was apologizing for the horse's erratic and less than efficient behavior. "He's young," the neighbor said, "and ain't been broke to the traces."

For the uninformed, that meant that the horse had not yet learned to respond properly to his harness and the reins that are ultimately attached to a metal bit in the horse's mouth. A tug on the reins to the left, for example, pulls the bit back in the horse's mouth on the left hand side, causing the horse to turn his head leftward to relieve the pain. His body and, subsequently, the plow follow the movement of the head. After going through this routine often enough with each tug on the reins, accompanied by the appropriate vocal command-- gee, haw, whoa--the poor horse finally learns that "gee" means you're going to get it on the right and "haw" means you're going to get it on the left if you don't make the right moves. "Whoa" means you better damn well stop in your tracks or you're going to get it from both directions.

Sooner or later even the dumbest horse is going to figure this out to the point that only the vocal command or perhaps the slightest touch on the reins will cause him to do what the man holding the reins wants done. He has then been "broke to the traces."

Throughout our own lives we wear our own harness and respond to our own learned commands to avoid the pain of wayward motions. The bit in our mouth is invisible but just as bruising when society, management, friends or lovers reject our actions. When we learn to do things the way they want them done, we can generally avoid physical pain and perhaps even receive the pleasure of some reward in the process.

The avoidance of physical pain, however, does not assure avoidance of mental pain--when the urge to resist, with its accompanying feelings of guilt or insufficiency, remains after the body has acquiesced.

Fortunately, when the mind needs that guidance or comforting, there are vast inventories of sage wisdom and advice one can key up in his mental computer to massage today's burdensome problems. I have refined mine down to a few that seems to help me sort through the conflicts and challenges of business as well as life in general. Some may appear to be contradictory but, as always, they only serve as reminders that problems usually have more than one solution.

My strongest guide is the Golden Rule. When people really practice it, the need for the others is lessened greatly. The problem is that all people do not "do unto you" the right way. That's when you may want to go ahead and turn the other cheek; just be ready to duck.

The second is the familiar *"God grant me the serenity to accept the things cannot change, the courage to change the things I can, and the wisdom to know the difference."* Wisdom, of course, is what we are looking for here, which is easier to seek than to find.

In Walter Foss Smith's poem, "The Calf Path" he describes human nature in tackling problems and their response to them. It is set against the natural development of an inefficient network of roads which begins:

"One day through a primeval wood
a calf walked home as good calves should
and made a trail all bent askew,
a crooked trail as all calves do."

Then the poem relates how other animals, seeking the easiest path already broken by the calf, followed in progressively larger species until it was ultimately used by man with his horse, wagon, cars and so on. Everyone cursed the crooked road although they were unconsciously following meanderings of an ancient calf. Near the conclusion, the poem contains my favorite verse.

"But men are prone to go it blind
along the calf path of the mind
and toil away from sun to sun
to do what other men have done."

Obviously we do not need to always be trying to reinvent the wheel but there are many times when our conditioned responses could stand a challenge. The easy way out is the way most chosen. And that's why these rules have become my favorites.

By the yard it's hard, by the inch it's a cinch.

When a big problem is tackled by breaking it down into parts and then solving these, somehow the problem doesn't seem as overwhelming. Progress can be measured, as reinforcement, along the way. Eventually the combined solution of the parts provides the success far too remote to hope for in the beginning when we looked at life "by the yard."

Let's think of a few reasons why it can be done.

Anybody can tell you why something can't be done. My most memorable and major successes have involved situations in which knowledgeable and capable professionals have assured me--no, guaranteed me--that what I wanted to do couldn't be done. This doesn't happen all the time but if I had taken their word for it, these successes wouldn't have happened at all.

Lead, follow, or get the hell out of the way.

I learned early in life that if you take a man's money, you ought to give him an honest day's work. The companion rule, *"If you have to do something, try to do it cheerfully,"* is sometimes harder to follow. A person can be productive and worth his pay even if he doesn't like what he is doing. The problem, however, is that misery with one's position or situation is usually counter productive and contaminates the spirit and performance of those surrounding him. If God doesn't either grant the serenity or push along a little change pretty soon that will make life more tenable, the wise choice would seem to be to get the hell out of the way. Life's too short to have to complain all the way through it. Besides, people get tired of hearing it anyway.

In my youth we had logging horses that we occasionally used to plow. Logging horses typically deal with a completely different set of circumstances in that they pull logs down a mountainside instead of a plow across relatively level ground. They learned, for example, that when slack occurred in their chains and they didn't feel the load, they better step aside. The logs behind them were moving faster than they were and even the sturdy shins of a logging horse were not going to stop their descent. The grab, or holding device, on the lead log was designed to pull out as the logs passed the horse, saving his shins and maybe his life. When that same horse was used to plow a field and something happened to cause the chain to slacken, the logging horse was likely to also step aside. This very sound reaction on a mountainside was frowned upon by the farmer who took pride in nice, straight furrows. On the other hand, I suspect that one or two good plow horses may have been lost over the years when pressed into service to pull logs down the side of a mountain. Both may have been "broke to the traces," but in different ways.

I felt that way when I made a mid-life career switch from lending to public accounting. In preparing for the change, I obtained an M.B.A. and passed the grueling Certified Public Accountant examination before I ever looked for a trainee position with an accounting firm. I knew that it would be difficult to find a job at my age unless I had impressive credentials and I needed the work experience to become certified. But until I joined the accounting firm, everything I knew came out of books. I had never worked a day in accounting in my life.

One of the first accounting jobs all trainee's face is reconciling a client's bank account. Usually these are fairly straightforward and clean, sometimes tedious and difficult, but not the biggest challenge in professional accounting by any means. I became stuck with one the first few days on the job that I still couldn't get to balance after several hours of work. The partner in charge began making frequent trips back and forth down the hall, glancing in as he passed my office with growing concern and frustration on his face.

Finally he came in, trying to keep his cool, and asked me how I was coming along. When I told him I was still out of balance and couldn't find the problem, he exploded.

After hearing what all was wrong with an educational system that could produce an M.B.A. with a 4.0 grade point average and a professional testing system that could allow a candidate to pass its entrance examination without being able to balance a simple bank account, I could tell he was not pleased with my performance.

As he wound down, I suggested to him that he was probably right and that I, too, was concerned with my inability to solve the problem within the normal half hour or so one might normally devote to a bank reconciliation. I further suggested that while his criticism helped vent his own frustrations, I seriously doubted that I had learned anything about a bank reconciliation from it, whereas I might if he would sit down with me and show me what I was doing wrong. He seemed a little shocked at first by my calm reaction to his reprimand but agreed to do just that.

It took both of us over two hours to find the very unique double error that was causing my problem. When it was over, the partner apologized for his earlier outburst and acknowledged that he would have been--and, in fact, was--as stymied as I had been with this particular problem. He had been away from the nitty gritty detail of accounting too long to remember that even the softest ground and smoothest fields contain a few heavy snags sometimes. The plow horse will stop and wait for a command. The logging horse will simply pull harder against the load. Both are only doing what they know best.

When I find myself in the changing harness of life, chewing on my invisible bit, and wondering where the next tug on the reins is coming from, I often think of those poor animals in their own changing world of expectations. At such times, it helps to have something to hang on to as a guide through the uncertainties of life. And change, each with its own new set of commands, may be the only true constant we face.

These, then, are the thoughts I lean on most. They apply to almost any circumstance and in a period of runaway logs or crooked furrows, somehow they help to cope.

In the long run, that may be the best we can hope for anyway.

ON ONE-ROOM SCHOOLS

In a way, going to a one-room school was like spending three years in the Army at the tail end of the Korean war. Both had their downside but the experience has lasted a lifetime.

There probably aren't any schools like mine that are left anymore, but some of the old buildings are still there - either falling down or converted into cheap living accommodations for somebody willing to fix them up. Someone lives in the one I attended back in the late forties; but, for the most part, the outside still looks the same. One of the two outhouses is gone and the old playground is grown up in weeds, but as I last stood there looking backward over those young years, everything else was as it always had been.

I could feel the cool freshness of the grass against my bare feet, which could move like they had wings, on that first warm day of spring when you finally could rid yourself of those heavy brogans of winter. I could taste the peppermint that grew wild in the lowlands beneath the road. And I could smell the musty, hand-soiled volumes of Tom Sawyer, Huckleberry Finn and other adventure stories from our tiny combination cloakroom-library. It was almost like nothing had changed when, in fact, the whole world had changed.

Modern schools appear to be more concerned with personal development than with the fundamentals of basic education. Class offerings, even at middle school level, sometimes include subjects such as interior decorating, horticulture, home economics and shop - all equally available to both genders. The objective seems to be the graduation of students who are well rounded, socialized individuals. So while we slide down the scale of the world's math and science scholarship, we are developing more sensitive and "better" people. One-room schools, of economic and logistical necessity, did things differently.

Through the fourth grade, I had attended a school in town with more kids in one class than were in the entire student population of Adkins Grade School. We were the casualties, or beneficiaries, of redistricting; my cousins, my brother and me. Up until then, we had to walk a mile in one direction to catch a bus to ride five more miles to town. After the redistricting, we had to walk a mile in the opposite direction to reach our new one room school.

My class now had four students in it, two boys and two girls. Three of us went on to complete high school. Two of us later completed college at night, eventually earning masters degrees, while working to support our families. Faye Kennedy became a teacher of gifted children. To my knowledge, we were two of only three students of Adkins Grade School to ever go on to college. The other preceded us by several years, becoming a medical doctor.

If you had known us then, you wouldn't have given any of us half a chance to even graduate high school. That's a pure and simple fact. You would have had to be there to understand.

We only had one teacher for all nine grades, which included primer in our vernacular. The school building was only about forty feet long by thirty feet wide, and part of that was taken up by two little rooms on each side of a recessed entrance. One was the cloakroom and library; the other was for our water urn, cleaning supplies and whatever else.

When you entered the building you faced a blackboard at the opposite end with the teacher's desk off to the left. Then there was a row of open seats facing the blackboard. This was where the class in session would sit when it was their turn for a lesson. Behind them, in four or five columns of six or seven desks, is where the students sat.

The schoolhouse was built on the side of a hill with windows only on the downhill side. Since we had no electricity, the windows were our major source of light. The youngest children were seated next to the windows, beginning with primer and continuing back and forth through each grade until you reached the right wall. That's where the oldest students sat. It was like the teacher was giving the little kids a goal to shoot for. They could start off with bright hopes and if they were able to progress steadily forward to the eighth and final grade, they would be completely in the dark.

That's facetious, of course, although the description is factual. In reality, however, the quality of basic education was good and it was hard not to learn. Each student was exposed to every lesson in every grade year, so if you missed something the year before or wanted to know what was coming next, all you had to do was pay attention to the class in session. By the time you got through the eighth grade, if you didn't know the capital of whatever country somebody mentioned, it was because someone had changed the name of the city or the country on you--which didn't happen nearly as often back then as it does now.

The problem with our education, some would argue, is that its scope and quality were necessarily limited by only having one teacher who was spread too thin to do a good job with any particular subject or class. All I know is that by the time I got to high school, I was as well equipped academically as anyone else.

What we were lacking, I suppose, were the athletic and social experiences of a larger school. Consolidation of the school system tried to cure that, and introduce other efficiencies at the same time. Up until then, the biggest problem was just getting to school from long distances with no transportation, which had to have had its impact on the high school dropout rate.

The very year after we graduated from the eighth grade, they started running school buses to remote areas and began school consolidation. Before that, for most people living farther away from the high school bus stop than we did, the eighth grade was about the extent of their education. The expanded bus transportation opened up new opportunities for everyone and led to the eventual closing of our one room school.

Getting back to the education, I think our teacher performed his teaching duties quite well and still found time to be human. With regard to socialization, ours was simply of a different variety. We were like one large family of twenty-five or thirty kids; the big kids taking care of the little kids and all of us looking out for each other.

We didn't have indoor plumbing so we had to carry water in buckets from a well about a quarter mile away. The school was heated in winter with one big pot bellied stove. Johnny Kennedy had the job of building the fire, having inherited it from an older brother. I think he was paid five dollars a month to build the fire, keep the stove cleaned out and bring in the coal. Since he had to be there before and leave after everybody else, he set and run trap lines to and from school. He trapped for beaver, mink and muskrats but he caught mostly muskrats. He tanned and sold their hides and made more money that way. If we had been smart enough to know what success was back then, we might have voted Johnny most likely to succeed. That would have probably ruined it for him though. I never saw it work for anyone else.

Our "athletics" involved games that everyone could play. We only had a little piece of bottomland and we played games like "base" and "round town" in the spring and fall. In the winter we played snow games like "fox and geese"

or rode our sleds. When we formed teams, we had two of the oldest boys as the captains and we chose up sides until all the kids who wanted to play were on one side or the other. My classmate and best friend, Tommy Cook, and I were almost always on opposite sides because we were the only two boys in our class and, consequently, in our age group. We learned to be competitive without letting it affect our friendship. But choosing sides is tough. Someone's feelings usually get hurt along the way. It doesn't sound much different from getting cut from a big city basketball team; but, in this case, it may happen every day and it's done to you by someone you know, trust and to whom you may be related. Don't expect any favors from someone who wanted to play on your team and got passed over for someone else's little brother.

We often created our own forms of diversion, like building a mud dam on the little branch that ran down to the creek beside the school. The teacher would sometimes let us stay out until the water could be contained no longer and the dam broke. That gave us great incentive to work together and work hard to keep the recess or lunch period going. Sometimes, when Janette came by, the teacher would even encourage us to build a dam and see how long we could keep it from breaking. Then he and Janette would go inside and lock the door. Since, as I said, all the windows were on the downhill side, we couldn't see in because it was too high from the ground up to the windows. We tried. We never knew for sure what they were doing in there. Somebody said the teacher was giving Janette private lessons. We wondered about that. She never seemed to have liked school all that much when she dropped out three or four years before.

Believe it or not, there was another one room school a few miles on farther up the creek. There used to be an old expression: "The farther up the hollow you go, the meaner the people get." I can attest to the fact that there was more than a ring of truth to it in this case. That little school had a terrible time keeping a teacher, partly because of its remote location and rough, unpaved road. The other "partly" may have been the real reason. We ventured up there one day to look at the tree where somebody said some of the boys had tried to hang their last teacher. They must have lived in the last house. Fortunately for her, some men happened by just in time to save her from probable death. The boys really weren't that mean; they were just a touch wild. We didn't go up there very often. Imagine, there we were living right on the fringe of civilization ourselves, thinking someone else was a touch wild.

That's why I said you had to have been there to know what it took for any of us to go on to high school and for Faye and me to go on to college. Most were like Tommy. Every time a logging truck would pass anywhere near where we were, Tommy would run to the road, making an arm motion that asked the driver to blow his air horns. Tommy loved those horns in a way that some people love train whistles, I guess. Maybe it's the sound of their own destiny they hear. During the year or two that Tommy attended high school he concentrated on vocational training. As soon as he could, he quit school and started driving a log truck. If I know Tommy, I bet it had plenty of air horns. That's what he loved. And driving a truck was what he always wanted to do.

That's what was really different about attending a one-room school. It gave you a chance to focus. You looked at basics and you learned them over and over until you knew them or tossed them aside completely. Then the focus was on getting married or driving a truck or whatever else you set your mind on instead.

I am not advocating a return to one-room schools but I do believe that the students of modern schools could benefit from that lost concentration and focus. That may be why home schooling is becoming more popular. While the underlying objectives of today's educational system may be admirable, it seems to me there is time to learn about interior decorating after a student has learned to be productive; and, earned enough money to have something to decorate. And I doubt that any of the students, over the age of ten, in our one room school didn't know how to pick, string and cook a pot of green beans - seasoned, no less, with a ham hock from the smoke house. They could even pick you a tomato or pull an onion to eat with them. Talk about home economics and horticulture.

More important, those old one room schools taught students what it takes to meet life's expectations, to work together, to take care of each other and to be content with the opportunities we have in life. Today, we tell every child that he or she can be President of the United States or whatever he or she wants to be if they try hard enough. That's okay; we were told that, too. But there apparently isn't much talk about the fact that there is only one President. Idealism and realism have to meet sometime. I think students would benefit, as well, by learning about the value and contributions of those at the bottom or the middle of the pyramid.

Tommy contributed by driving his log truck that ultimately supplied the mines with the needed timbers, which kept more highly paid people employed. Virginia Johnson, the fourth member of our class, also followed her dreams. She graduated from high school; got married; became a life-long, supportive member of her church and her community; and, parented and raised children who are making their own contributions to society.

The virtues and values learned in our one room school helped pave the way for each of us to choose a path in life based upon our own personal level of ambition, energy, responsibility and satisfaction. There is no shame or sacrifice in that. A child can learn a lot from building mud dams.

Looking back, I think that Mr. Walker, our teacher, did an admirable job with the resources he had. With their far more abundant resources, I am glad that modern educators seek to arouse the curiosity and excite the imagination of their students beyond what he was able to do. I just hope, at the same time, they make sure they are providing the real fundamentals and focus that builds true equality of opportunity. Without that foundation, those young dreams they inspire will be like clouds, and will evaporate just as quickly in the shifting winds of change.

ON SMALL BLESSINGS

She waited at the mailbox, her Scooby-Doo overnight bag firmly in hand. She was five years old and had already called Mommaw to see if she could spend the night. Mommaw, of course, said "yes', but she asked Sarah to wash her hands and face, and to brush her hair and to put on her shoes, before Mommaw got there to pick her up. Then they could stop by KFC on the way back to pick up Sarah's favorite supper.

So when Mommaw got there, Sarah was standing by the mail box, hands washed, faced washed, hair brushed; and, bag packed with everything but what she might need to spend the night. That didn't matter. Mommaw already had all that.

When she saw Sarah, tears rolled down Mommaw's cheeks. Since the divorce proceedings, she hadn't seen nearly as much of Sarah as she had the first four years of her life. Photo album after photo album, and a stack of home movies, told the story of how she had kept Sarah from infancy until kindergarten. The bond between them had become as strong as that of any mother and child. Then came kindergarten and Sarah wasn't there as much anymore. Then came the divorce and Sarah was caught in the middle of something she didn't make; something she didn't understand. Mommy and Daddy didn't like each other anymore and she had lost familiar access to everyone else who meant anything to her, except her older brother and sister. They, however, had friends near their own age - eight and nine - who helped keep them occupied. But there were no children of Sarah's age in their new subdivision. And, recently, even her cat had died.

On this Friday evening, she was feeling alone and hungry. She called Mommaw to see if she could spend the night. And Mommaw wasted no time in going to get her.

When she arrived at the house, she rushed to Poppaw's anxious arms for a hug and a brief stay in the comfort of his lap. Then she ate supper: chicken legs, mashed potatoes and gravy, biscuit and chocolate milk. After supper, she turned to her doll houses, still where they were when she last played with them, and spent at least the next hour with her favorite toys. After that, Mommaw gave her a warm bath, dressed her in new pajamas she had just bought for her, and then took her tired little body to bed. Mommaw lay beside her, gently rubbing her back as Sarah often asked her to do, and in minutes she was sound asleep.

So there lay Sarah, asleep in Mommaw's bed, her back having been rubbed with the loving tenderness that only Mommaw knew how to do. Safe from the family discord. Away from the yelling and screaming, accusations and crying, verbal attacks and counter attacks, which disturb and frighten young minds. For the moment, she was at peace with the world. And at that moment, whether she felt it or not, she was deeply, deeply loved.

Mommaw and Poppaw, who have been married for the better part of fifty years, do not understand what makes two handsome, well educated people, with brilliant careers and three beautiful children, call it quits. Whatever their expectation of marital bliss might have been during their sixteen years together, in the end, they obviously didn't find it.

But this evening, for Sarah, in the midst of all the trauma, there is a brief reprieve. She is asleep in Mommaw's bed, curled tightly against the one person she knows will hold her, protect her and love her. She is spending the night with Mommaw, where there will be no signs of animosity or anger or the pulling apart of a young family's lives.

And, for now at least, there is no thought of tomorrow and what that will bring. Tonight, she is with Mommaw and Poppaw. In a small world turned upside down, it is what comforts her most. Not what was expected only a year earlier, and certainly not what any of them deserved; but, for tonight, with Sarah safe and happy again - and Mommaw and Poppaw comforted in that knowledge - it was a small blessing for all three.

ON OUT-OF-BODY EXPERIENCES

I alluded to an out-of-body experience in my perspective, On Religion, but without explanation. This is what happened.

It was probably January or February of 1965. We had already moved into our new house on Ridgeway Drive in Jeffersonville, Indiana and had become frustrated over the lack of attention that C.A.G. Corporation, our builder, was paying to the several defects and omissions that we had discovered in the construction of our house. It may have been too early for the sod to be delivered for our lawn, but the other things, such as failing to anchor the non-locking side of our patio doors, should have been corrected by then.

I went down to the sales office, located in the first house on the left as one entered the subdivision; parked my car outside the office; and, stepped out onto a sidewalk covered with ice. The leather soles and heels of my shoes provided no traction and I fell - feet flying forward, body and head flying backward - as my consciousness failed me.

I don't know how much time had expired before I was aware that I was floating above my body, looking down at the back of the heads of some three people who had gathered around me trying to resuscitate my lifeless body. No one was around when I fell and I can only assume that my accident was observed from the office and that help emanated from there.

From my floating position, I could see my face, but felt no emotion about that being I being administered to. I was totally calm, totally at peace, and had become what one might describe as a disinterested observer. Then it was over; I regained consciousness and looked up into the faces of my caregivers. I could feel severe pain in my side and back.

The builder sent me to the firm's doctor who examined me and told me that I had suffered some bruised ribs. It took several weeks to get over the pain. A couple of years later, while undergoing a physical examination, the examining physician asked me how I had suffered the broken ribs that his xray had detected. Apparently they had healed irregularly and I will never know what other damage they may have done at that time.

But I do know this. That accident took me to somewhere I had never been before. There were no bright lights, no tunnels, no music as others have described in what they term "near death experiences." So I won't call mine that. But it was out-of-body and it was real. It made me see life and death in a way I had never seen it before.

Quite frankly, no further interpretation is necessary.

ON LEPRECHAUNS

I've never seen a live leprechaun. In fact, my mind is still healthy enough to know that they don't exist. Even my Irish heritage has been watered down with enough English, Scottish and Germanic bloodlines that whatever is left wouldn't be enough to really claim. Yet, I have heard of people who still believe leprechauns do exist and swear by their secret powers and wisdom. I also have heard that, despite their mischievous nature, they are extremely loyal to those who do believe in them and treat them right. Folklore admits that they are not easily caught, but if you do catch one, it can reveal hidden treasures to you.

Maybe that's why, when I saw Darby in a novelty catalog several years ago, I couldn't resist sending for him - although I rarely purchase anything by mail.

When Darby arrived, he was less than six inches long, dressed in top hat and customary leprechaun garb, lying on his side - one hand holding up his hat and face and the other firmly grasping a piece of the Blarney Stone. His cragged face was softened by a wry little smile and, from my desk that he chose as his place of repose, his knowing eyes kept watch as I went about my routine activities.

Early on, after he arrived, when I made a particular decision that Elizabeth questioned me about, I would jokingly say, "Darby helped me with the answer." She laughed - especially when the decision turned out to be one with which she agreed. More often than not, they were good decisions.

77

As years went on, when I approached another difficult decision, I found myself looking at Darby.

"Oi see ye've got another brain twister." he would seem to say.

"Yes," I mentally responded, "but I'm down to two or three alternatives and I'm not quite sure yet which way to go."

"Well, kin ye stoke up yer pipe and share a waft of that fine smoke wi' me while we ponder this over?" I would seem to glean from his wistful eyes.

Then as I edged closer and closer to a decision, both of us enjoying the haze of tobacco smoke - decidedly unhealthy for me, perhaps, but not seeming to bother Darby in the least - I would apparently relax in the comfort of a final choice.

When I would glance down at Darby, that sly little smile said it all. "Ah, oi see ye've figgered it oate fer yersef" in the heaviest Irish brogue I could imagine.

And, indeed, I had ... decision after decision, over the years that brought me more than my share of prosperity, health and happiness.

As those years went by, when Elizabeth asked me how I came to a particular decision we both thought was important, and I invoked Darby's name, somewhere during that time she quit laughing.

I don't know whether she, finally, had come to believe in leprechauns or not. But, not long ago, she went out shopping and, when she came back, she had caught one of her own.

ON INDIVIDUAL RIGHTS

This is a sore subject with me.

When my children were teenagers in the 1970's, all I seemed to hear, whenever they were denied any privilege, was: "I have my rights!"

I told them one day that if they thought they had rights: go down to the back streets some night; walk up a dark alley; and, explain their rights to the first hoodlum they met who was ready to beat their brains out.

Obviously I did not want either of them to get hurt, but it irks me no end that people don't seem to understand that "rights" are not something that comes out of the womb with you as a protective coating. They are the brilliant and idealistic gifts of our founding fathers who, themselves, had earned them and who knew that the rights they proclaimed would never survive without the protection by those willing to do whatever it takes to preserve them. That means people putting themselves in harm's way, too often resulting in death and all the lesser sacrifices they might make, to preserve the values and security of our families, our communities, and our country.

Yet, there are those who, like my children, never seem to understand that we, as individuals, have no rights except for those that are given to us and protected by others. Simply put, the weak have no rights except for the compassion and sense of duty of the strong.

That's why this subject is a sore spot with me. Far too many individuals and organizations lean much too heavily on the assertion of their "rights" as they go about abusing them. To them, the end justifies the means. Some are more than willing to step all over other innocent people in order to promote a selfish interest. I will never appreciate the logic, or understand the vengeance, of those who would drive a metal spike into a tree for the sole purpose of maiming or killing some hapless logger, working for minimum wage to support his family. There is nothing noble or righteous in that.

Don't get me wrong; I'm for treating all people humanely and justly. It is the whiners and the abusers who are always trying to stretch the blanket for their own myopic purposes to the detriment of others that I can't stand.

I served in the military at the end of the Korean Conflict, spending two years overseas. I was never in combat but I had four brothers who were, during World War II. One did not survive. Two others served in Korea, one during the conflict and one during the peacekeeping mission afterwards. Many of those individuals who loudly proclaim - and demand protection for - their own individual rights would not have given any of them the time of day. More likely, they would have ridiculed them - in some safe forum, of course - for being stupid enough to join the military services in the first place.

The veterans of Viet Nam certainly know that feeling and, no doubt, many members of the current military, police, fire and other protective services have felt under-appreciated by those they are duty bound to serve and protect.

During my college years, we were required to read a book titled "Centuries of Childhood" by an author whose name I no longer remember. But the message remains clear. The book described the various roles that children have played throughout history, on an ever-swinging pendulum. In some ages, they were doted upon and treated like the masters of the universe; at other times, they were abused and forced to do indescribable things. It was all documented in that book, with the pendulum continuing to swing. As individuals, we are all "children", subject to the whims and tolerances of the greater society in which we live.

Someday, even here in America, unless the strong and compassionate continue to fight for the weak - and the weak minded - there may no longer be any "rights" except those which each person can carve out for himself. And, it takes more than writing on a piece of paper to do that.

Too bad for those who don't seem to comprehend or appreciate this fact. To me, it seems simple enough.

ON CRYPTIC MESSAGES

Several years ago, while on a rare trip to my hometown in West Virginia, I visited the cemetery where my parents and two brothers were buried. After noting the deteriorating condition of the headstones on my parents' and one brother's graves, I vowed to replace all of them the first chance I got and to put a permanent marker on the unmarked grave of the second brother who was stillborn in 1939 and given only a temporary marker. That project, unfortunately, went the way of many good intentions until much later when my resolve finally caught up with my feelings of guilt.

The first thing I learned, when I contracted with a company in the area to supply the monuments, was that the temporary marker on the stillborn baby's grave was gone. They could not be certain of his gravesite. I then contacted two older sisters and a younger brother - my only surviving siblings - to explain my intentions, get their approval and advice, and to see if they could identify the exact location of the unmarked grave. All expressed appreciation for, and approval of, the project but none were absolutely certain about the gravesite.

My oldest sister, Marie, however, threw me a real curve: she asked me to add a memorial stone for another brother who had been declared "missing in action" during World War II and whose body was never recovered; and, she asked me to fulfill a deathbed promise she had made to our mother to place a headstone on the grave of her first son and our oldest brother, Sebastian, who had died of a childhood disease, at age 8, in 1923. This was years before I was born and, to complicate matters further, he had been buried in another state. The real obstacle to this request, however, was that the town in which Sebastian was buried - Azen, Virginia - no longer existed. I had only the extremely vague memory of Marie, now eighty years old and in poor health, to guide me in the right direction.

My next steps were to enlist the assistance of someone I knew in each of the areas where the graves were located - both remote to me - who might help me find the precise locations of the two unmarked graves, if it could be done at all. That help came in the form of a former classmate, Faye Kennedy, in West Virginia and a cousin, Cecil Hensley, who lives at Whitetop, Virginia near where Azen used to be. Both enthusiastically endorsed the project and did excellent investigative work to pursue the answers.

In Faye's case, being a schoolteacher who had remained in our small hometown all her life, she used her knowledge of families with loved ones buried in the same West Virginia cemetery to locate older survivors still in the area. Among them was one who still had a handwritten copy of a cemetery plat, which had been prepared by interested parties many years ago. My brother, Benjamin Raymond, occupied an unmarked site beside my mother's grave. It actually was where my sister thought it should be, but the guesswork had now been eliminated.

Cecil's challenge in Virginia was more difficult. He was able to locate the church and cemetery where Sebastian was known to have been buried; but the cemetery had sixteen unmarked graves. Any one of them could have been my brother's. It had been nearly eighty years since Sebastian had been buried there and no one alive had any clue as to the location of his grave.

I remembered that Ethan, my younger brother, had sent me some old photographs and other souvenirs a year or so earlier, that Marie had given him to pass on to other family members in anticipation of what she considered to be her impending death. In my research of these and other items, I found a very old and frayed family Bible. On one of the pages, presumably in the only sample I have of my mother's handwriting, were the directions to Sebastian's grave, including the name of the person buried beside him. This information enabled Cecil and the cemetery's caretaker to locate the exact place where Sebastian was buried.

The company with whom I had contracted for monuments in West Virginia had designed polished granite headstones for me, which included a special insignia - the last letter of our surname enclosed in a shield at the top center of the stone. I had requested them to be dignified but not overwhelming, out of respect for others - including distant relatives and friends - buried in these small, family cemeteries. I shared their design with the Virginia supplier. They duplicated the stone and the style of inscribed personal information so that, even though the graves in West Virginia and Sebastian's grave in Virginia were located some two hundred miles apart, these members of our family were joined together in the similarity of monuments that marked their places of rest.

On the day that I received photographic proof of installation of the last monument, I can't explain the sense of relief and fulfillment that I felt. The project had been completed. My brother, Paul, who gave his life as an airman over the Pacific Ocean in World War II, had been appropriately remembered and a deathbed promise that my sister had made to our mother nearly fifty years ago had been fulfilled. And, except to my siblings and me, it all would mean little to anyone else.

Yet, as I went downstairs to my basement office, at the bottom of the stairs I felt something near my foot. I accidentally kicked it before I noticed that it was a rose. Elizabeth had decorated the dining room for Valentine's Day only a few days before, using those same types of roses, and I decided she must have dropped one. But the dining room is upstairs, away from the stairway; the office carpet is a shade of off-white; and, the rose was deep red with dewdrops glistening on its petals. Why hadn't I noticed it before?

I picked up the rose and put it on my desk. As I looked at it, I thought of the only picture I have of my mother who died - at age 42 - when I was only seven. To the best of my knowledge, it is the only photograph taken of her during the last twenty years of her life. And like my memories of her from childhood, it is slightly out of focus. But, she is there, standing beside her beloved rose bushes in our front yard.

The rose on my office carpet surely got there by accident; and, it was only coincidental that it was discovered on that white carpet the very day that the monument project was completed. Had to be. A less pragmatic person, or a more spiritual person, may have thought it was some sort of cryptic message from beyond. I, of course, know better.

But, on the slightest chance I could be wrong:

You're welcome, Mom.

ON GRANDCHILDREN

Someone once quipped: "If I had known grandchildren were so much fun, I would have had them first." As most grandparents know, of course, you get to send the little tykes home when the fun begins to ebb a bit. Someone else has the more arduous responsibilities of keeping them bathed, fed, clothed, sheltered, educated, disciplined, and entertained along with the countless other scraps of daily maintenance which begins at birth and continues throughout life. Grandparents, of course, often share in these activities to varying degrees but, by and large, it is the shinier moments that bring us our happiness and light.

Our two children each provided us with three delightful grandchildren. Charlie has three boys: Branden, Logan and Justin. Sharon has one boy and two girls: Daniel, Kristen and Sarah. The only thing they have in common is the differences the two sets of cousins have among themselves. Yet, there is something strikingly similar as each set is compared with the other. The two oldest cousins, Branden and Daniel, are athletic although one prefers ice hockey and the other soccer. The two middle cousins, Logan and Kristen, are sensitive and artistic. Justin and Sarah, the youngest cousins, both have a boisterous bravado about them that separates, quickly and emphatically, what is important to them and what is not. For Justin, at age four, hitting a baseball off a tee was "sissy" and he refused to play the game until some real pitcher was throwing his best stuff at him. Sarah, at about the same age, got mad at me one day and began reciting the names of all the people and pets she loved, with my name conspicuously absent. When I jokingly asked her if that meant she didn't love me anymore, she said: "I love you, but I don't love you too much." The unique phrasing of her answer lingered with me for a year or so before "Too Much" was finished and became one of the more appreciated songs that I have ever written.

Kristen and Sarah always liked to sit with me to color, watch TV, read to me, and take an occasional nap or just talk about whatever they had on their minds at the time. This special bonding became the inspiration for another of my favorite songs, "Grand Daddy's Chair." The girls both loved that song and each received an autographed CD by the vocalist who did the beautiful demo. Their grandmother thought it was good but premature. She thought I should have waited until I died before I wrote it. Tough call.

Even at their young ages, all of my grandchildren have found ways to surprise me in one way or another. Dan, after making terrible grades in the fifth grade, found his focus to become a Dean's List student with an invitation to join the Junior Honor Society in the sixth grade. Branden became a traveling member of Louisville's junior ice hockey team. Kristen was invited to participate in a special art class for gifted students. Sarah and Justin are beginning to show the same signs of special achievement and may well surpass their siblings in whatever interests they develop. Logan, also an honor student in the second grade, has already done something quite memorable.

On Fathers' Day, 2002, which also coincided with my birthday, Logan handed me a personal gift. It was all of his allowance he had saved that week, amounting to eighty-eight cents. The reason I know how much it was is that I still have it all - with not one penny spent - in my desk. I thanked him at the time for his gift; but I also wrote him a personal letter, which I mailed to him the following day. Sheryl, his mother, told me afterwards that my letter to him is one of his most prized possessions. I was pleased to hear that, of course, but I know, down deep in my heart, it could never be worth three quarters, a dime and three pennies. That's a very special treasure. Allowance or not, I know where Logan's gift to me really came from that day.

ON OLD JOKES

When my grandson, Dan, first graced the hallowed halls of St. Anthony's as a precocious first grader, he took with him his mischievous and playful personality. That which was sometimes admired - or at least, tolerated - at home was not nearly as well accepted by his teachers; and, family members were recruited to help modify his classroom behavior. I had my grandfatherly talk with him one day and told him, of course, that he had to be good. I vividly recall his exasperated response: "I can't be good ALL the time!" So sayeth a first grader; so could say us all.

As I wind down to the end of my own personal challenges with life, I find that I am not too careful, myself, as I take an inventory of the good and the bad. But I reluctantly admit that I like old jokes. The few that I have tried to salvage here are some of my favorites from those stories I have used in training seminars or speeches back in the days when the audiences were generally all male and a little humor was expected if you wanted to hold their attention. Back then, of course, we were not hampered by political correctness or aware of our lack of sensitivity to ethnicity, gender, race, religion, sexual preference, animals, plants, microbes and all other living organisms. I have culled out many of those old stories so as to not offend any more people than I had to, but Dan was right. You can't be good all the time.

My first impulse was to tell you how and why I had used these stories but I toned that down quite a bit. Just as I did with the course language where I could. As a further accommodation to thoughtful and busy people who may only be interested in the jokes and can live without all of the connecting verbiage, I have even separated the jokes from other narrative by asterisks. So if you want to cut to the chase, just read between the asterisks. But if you are in an airplane, on a cruise ship, or are a passenger in a car going through the construction around Louisville or Nashville, you may as well go ahead and read the whole thing. You've got plenty of time.

My first old joke is one that gained a famous comedian some additional notoriety for his "spontaneous wit", simply because he recycled it, changing the setting to flowers in a flowerpot. I mention this only for those who may be looking for some redeeming value in an otherwise inane look back at what an older generation called humor. Putting all this in a historical perspective, instead of just laughing, may provide that needed, and less embarrassing, purpose. Almost everyone can appreciate history.

*****

A lion tamer had, as part of his act, his most ferocious looking lion approach this beautiful woman who had entered the cage, and appear to kiss her on the mouth.

Amidst the applause that followed this sensational act came the loud, boisterous voice of an obvious drunk in the audience repeatedly saying. "That's not so great. I can do that. That's not so great."

The lion tamer, becoming irritated, invited the drunk to come down and try it. His invitation was met by total silence. "Well," he said. "Are you coming down or not?"

"Sure, I will." yelled back the drunk. "But, get that damned lion out of there."

*****

I have recycled a lot of old material myself for the purpose of illustrating certain points. The next one tells you how even small distractions can cost you dearly.

*****

Two men were shooting dice on the street corner when they were approached by a gorgeous young woman who wanted to know if she could play too. They said she could if she had the money. She reached in her purse, pulled out a few dollars, dropped them on the street, squatted down in a very unladylike manner, rolled the dice one time, picked up all the money and walked away.

One of the men looked at the other and said, "Did you see what she rolled?" to which his friend responded in total bewilderment,

"Hell NO! Did YOU?"

*****

I always liked jokes like that. The ones that help you make a point. Here's one that emphasizes the power of motivation.

A patron of the local pub staggered home late one night, missed his turn and passed briefly through the cemetery until he fell into an uncovered grave freshly dug for a burial scheduled the next day. Frantic at first, he dug and clawed trying to get out but the hole was too deep. He even got back as far as he could to take a run and jump to grab for the top. Still no luck. Finally, in total exhaustion, he gave up and decided to sit back in one corner until daybreak so he could get some help. Just then another drunk, apparently taking the same path, also fell in the grave. Startled initially, the first man cowered silently and unnoticed as he watched the second man go through all the same vain efforts to remove himself from the grave. Then, just as the

second drunk backed up to take his run and go at jumping up and out, the first man broke the darkened silence: "Bet you can't make it."

He did!

Other of those old jokes can help place a good-natured focus on just about anything. Here's a few that I have used to stress the power of observation, enlightenment and the value of good old fashion trust.

*****

Things were pretty quiet at the hospital and one of the doctors was walking down the hallway when he happened to notice a man draped over one of the chandeliers. There was a janitor in the same general area with his mop and pail, busily cleaning the floors and apparently paying no attention to anything else. The doctor walked over to him, interrupted him and pointed up to the man on the chandelier. "What's that guy doing up there?" the doctor asked. "He thinks he's a light bulb," the janitor replied. "Sad!" commented the doctor. "Come on. Help me get him down and I'll take him back to the psychiatric ward and see if we can't get him some treatment." After they got a ladder and untangled the poor man from the chandelier, the doctor started with him down the hall when he noticed that the janitor had picked up his bucket and mop and was following him.

"That's okay," said the doctor, "I can take it from here. You go on back to work."

"Back to work! You've got some nerve!" the janitor exclaimed. "Here you come and take down the light bulb and now you expect me to work back there in the dark!"

*****

While he was out for a late evening walk through the woods, a hiker found himself in almost total darkness. Despite feeling his way carefully along the narrow mountain path, he eventually slipped and fell over what appeared to be a cliff. As he fell, he managed to grab onto a small shrub that broke his fall; however, he felt nothing under him and was not able to pull himself up to a safe location. Peering upward through the darkness, his fear and instincts caused him to call for help.

"Anyone up there?" he yelled.

To his surprise, he was answered by a deep, booming voice that said: "I am here for you, my son."

"Can you get me out of here?" the fallen man nervously asked.

"Do you trust me?" the booming voice asked.

"Yes", the fallen man replied.

"Then let go of the branch."

An awkward moment of silence passed before the hiker spoke again.

"Anybody else up there?"

*****

There are people who are genuinely offended by stories that smack of anything crude or politically incorrect. The next one is both. Back in my less sensitive days, I used it to try to get branch managers more involved in the training of their employees. That's all history now, of course.

A young mountain woman appeared at one of the Appalachian Regional Hospitals for some free health counseling and approached the receptionist. "I'd like to see an upturn." she said. The receptionist looked her over coldly and replied. "You mean an intern, don't you, honey?"

"I guess so," the mountain woman said, "I need a contamination."

The receptionist, with growing disdain, responded "That's examination you want, isn't it, dearie?"

Growing somewhat irritated with the tone of the conversation, the mountain woman replied:

"Look, intern, upturn, contamination, examination; what the hell's the difference. All I know is I ain't demonstrated in three months and I think I'm stagnant!"

*****

Some might say that was truly stupid and disgusting, but demonstration is an important training tool. When you don't regularly demonstrate the proper techniques for whatever you are trying to teach your people, you - and they - can become stagnant. This may be a challenged rationale today, but not back then when the audience was all men and you could get your message across with stories like that. Today people revel in the crudeness and stupidity that reigns on television but become very sensitive to whatever is said to a live mixed audience outside of a comedy club. Same people; different mindset.

Sometimes, though, a good joke is a good joke and the reliance on a particular word or situation is too important to attempt substitution. The next joke is one in which substitution just wouldn't work at all. So I warn you in advance. The critical word is that vulgar, gutter description of a necessary bodily function that some writers try to clean up by using "sh-". I wrestled with myself about doing the same thing. But I thought if you're going that far, why be hypocritical or timid about it? In my case, it was my wife. She said clean it up or take it out. So I made it as clean as I could. Anyway, here it is, sh-! and all..

*****

A crude, obnoxious patient was making a real nuisance of himself when the head nurse came in and demanded to know what was the matter. "I've got to sh-," he said.

"You can't use that foul language around here," she told him, "or you're going to end up swimming in your own manure."

Then after a few more choice words about his manners and upbringing, she suggested he describe his needs as a bowel movement or urination. When this didn't go over too well, she came to the conclusion that if he were going to act like a child, she would treat him like one. She spent the next few minutes educating him on the use of Number One and Number Two for those times when he needed a bedpan or a urine bottle.

Everything went well until they brought in another patient who suddenly had a severe attack of undetermined origin. The new patient lay in the next bed, screaming and moaning as doctors and nurses surrounded him trying to find out what was wrong. Meanwhile, the first patient, from his own bed, was smiling smugly and occasionally yelling out: "I know what's wrong with him!"

Finally, in frustration, one of the doctors snapped, "Okay, if you're so damned smart, what's wrong with him?"

"He's got to sh-", the first patient proudly exclaimed, "only he ain't got no number!"

*****

If you let temptation override your better judgment and read it anyway, you deserve to know that that joke has always been extremely popular with accountants. That may be good information. Accountants don't laugh all that much.

Doctors, lawyers and bankers have been associated with their own share of old jokes, too. Being a former banker, I like this one that involves all three.

An elderly man who had accumulated substantial wealth was near death and, ignoring the old saying that you can't take it with you, decided he wanted to try. He withdrew his money in cash, totaling $600,000, and called his doctor, lawyer and banker to his bedside. He explained his intentions and acknowledged that although he didn't really trust any of them, he didn't know anyone else he could call on to fulfill his wish. He gave them each $200,000 to secretly place in his casket after he was gone. After the old man died, the doctor started thinking about all the treatment he had given this particular old gentleman over the years, which probably prolonged his life. Finally, he decided that promise or not, he was entitled to at least $50,000 of the money and so, when the time came, he only put $150,000 in the casket.

The lawyer, it turns out, had wrestled with the same opportunity and being a little more larcenous by trade, settled on $100,000 as his fair compensation. They all met at the graveside and after the service, the doctor began to feel pangs of remorse. With the three of them together, he emotionally confessed what he had done. The lawyer broke down as well and then the two of them turned to the banker who couldn't believe his ears.

"I'm embarrassed and ashamed of you. Two highly regarded professionals!" he admonished. "I can't believe that either of you would break a deathbed promise to a man who trusted you as much as he did."

The lawyer, fighting back, said, "You mean to tell me that you, a banker of all people, put all that money down in that grave?"

"Damn right, I did!" the banker replied indignantly, pointing down. "It's right there in the casket. Wrote a check for the whole $200,000!"

*****

Back to raunchy or suggestive language, the next story also lacks opportunity for substitution, but fortunately it is a little more tender and compassionate than most. It tells of a tiny, gnarled little tree that stood on the edge of the forest, growing older and more self-conscious as the years went by when those passing would stop to look it over, wondering what kind of tree it was and often making uncomplimentary remarks about its appearance and possible origin. One day the little tree could stand it no longer and raised its frail, crooked branches in a plaintive plea to the large, handsome oak nearby.

"Tell me, Mr. Oak. You're a wise, old tree and I just have to know. What kind of tree am I? Am I a son of a beech? Am I a son of a birch...just what kind of tree am I?"

To which the wise old oak fondly and affectionately replied,

"No, my son, I regret to tell you that you are not a son of a beech and you're not a son of a birch. But I can tell you one thing. Your mother was one of the finest pieces of ash in this neck of the woods!"

★★★★★

Some jokes require dialects or body motion - in this case, rowing a boat - which doesn't seem to come across that well on paper. Just use your imagination as you consider the poor guy's plight.

Pierre, the lighthouse keeper, had been stationed out on that rocky little crag of an off-shore island for years, with only his beautiful young wife for comfort, and it had finally taken its toll. Late one evening, his wife looked out the window and saw Pierre quietly rowing his boat out into the water, heading for land. "Pierre," she yelled. "Where air you going?" Pierre looked back sullenly, continuing to row, and said, "I hate zis place. I leave zis place and I nevair come back!"

"But Pierre," his wife calls back, "What about zee lighthouse? Who weel take care of zee lighthouse?"

"Screw zee lighthouse!" Pierre replies, still rowing toward land, "I leave zis place and I nevair come back!"

"But Pierre," his wife pleads again, "What about zee ships? Zey come in zee night, zey crash on zee rocks. "

"Screw zee ships," Pierre retorts, still rowing toward land, " I leave zis place and I nevair come back!"

"But Pierre," his wife tries again, throwing off her robe and exposing her beautiful body in the brilliant moonlight, reflected even stronger by the sea. "What about me?"

"Dammit, woman," Pierre reluctantly responds, as he shifts directions and starts rowing back to the lighthouse, "Someday I gonna leave zis place and I nevair come back!"

*****

Another problem with old jokes, of course, is relevancy in our changing times. No one tells traveling salesmen jokes anymore because now, with wall-to-wall motels and rapid transit systems, salesmen are more likely to spend their evenings in the bar at Holiday Inn than they are to stop off at some old farmhouse to see if they can spend the night. Too bad. Those situations generated some unusual stories but I am going to include only one - purely for its historical perspective.

*****

A traveling salesman arrived at a farmhouse very late and prevailed upon the generosity of the farmer for overnight accommodations. The only available bed space in the house was with Grandpa who was already asleep. The salesman was really tired so he eagerly accepted their hospitality. He also took great care to not awaken Grandpa as he undressed and found his way to bed in the dark. He slept soundly until early the next morning when he was awakened by the excited and joyous appeal from beside him in the bed.

"Yippee, bring on the women! I'm young again, bring on the women!" The salesman, jerking upright in the bed, was not amused.

"Look, old man," he said, "What you have in your head is yours but what you have in your hand is mine!"

*****

Depression and recession also provide background for timely jokes. Like the man who had just lost his job and because of that misfortune, his wife and his car. The house was about the last thing to go and he was desperately trying to hang on to it. He grew a garden and sold the harvest and was almost able to see daylight in making his house payment, as he set out walking door-to-door to sell his last crop of strawberries. At the very first house, the young pretty housewife answered the door dressed only in a flimsy negligee. After a few moments of awkward conversation, the young woman said suggestively, "I don't have any money but I sure would like to have some of those strawberries. Isn't there anything else I could give you for them" The poor man started to cry. That startled the woman.

"Why all the tears?" she asked.

"Well," he said, "I've already lost my job, my wife and my car. I'm just about ready to lose my house. It seems like almost everything is already gone and now you're getting ready to screw me out of my strawberries."

*****

Relax. The worst is passed. The rest are a few disjointed stories that don't have any redeeming value at all. I just thought. . . Okay, consider it another history lesson.

A young country boy walked into the general store and asked the owner if he had any two by fours. The owner said that he did depending on how long he wanted them. The boy ran back outside and returned just a few minutes later with the answer.

"Daddy says he wants them for a long time. He's building a barn."

*****

A hold-up man was working a resort motel and happened to pick on a room occupied by a couple of newlyweds, married just that afternoon with barely enough time to get to their rooms. He burst in, mean looking and brandishing a pistol, and demanded all their money. But then he saw the bride, standing in the bathroom in her nightgown, getting ready for her new husband. As soon as he saw her, the hold-up man changed his mind and decided to force himself upon the young bride instead. Not having anything to tie the husband with, and since he wasn't getting much of a fight out of him anyway, the hold-up man simply drew an imaginary circle around him on the carpet and, in his meanest voice said, "I'll shoot you in a minute if you move one foot out of that circle!" After he had satisfied his lust and left, the young woman was understandably upset. "What kind of man did I marry? You let that creep attack me, and you just stood there! You didn't do ANYTHING!"

"Shoot!" said the husband. "That's all you know! While he wasn't looking, I stuck my foot out of the circle!"

*****

After going through a line at a crowded cafeteria, three rambunctious teenagers found they were forced to share a table with a kindly looking old lady. They wanted the table to themselves so one of the boys, nudging his friend underneath the table, suddenly remarked, "Did your mom and dad ever get married?" "Naw," replied his friend, picking up on the put-on. "How about yours?" Before the first one could answer, the third chimed in. "That's nothing. My mom doesn't even know who my old man is." At which point the little old lady looked up and said very sweetly,

"Excuse me, but would one of you little bastards please pass the sugar?"

*****

An old prospector was tying his mule to the hitching rack when a young half drunk cowboy came out of the saloon looking for a little fun. "Hey, old man," he asked the prospector, "Did you ever learn how to dance?"

He then began shooting at the old fellow's boots and laughing feverishly as the prospector tried to dodge the bullets. When the cowboy's gun was empty, the prospector reached across his mule, pulled a shotgun from its scabbard, and pointed it at his protagonist. "Well, son," he drawls, "now that I've learned to dance, I have a question for you. Have you ever kissed a mule's ass?"

The cowboy looked at the gun, looked at the mule, then looked at the prospector. "No, sir," he says, "but I sure always wanted to!"

*****

Okay, that's enough. What you missed, if you're wondering, is only a bunch of old ethnic jokes, or ones about old man-young woman romances, girls on bicycles, talking parrots or about things like the poor snake family that didn't have a pit to hiss in. I'll just finish by drawing upon the analogy used in the story, *The Danger of Innocence,* written, I believe, by the French author, Honore de Balzac. There, as I recall, a young man raised in a monastery was united with a young woman of equally sheltered background in an arranged marriage. The author compared their awkward attempts at consummation to that of a gorilla, tossed ashore from a shipwreck onto an island where he saw, for the first time, a coconut. Near starvation, he grabs the coconut, sniffing it, tossing it, squeezing it: he knows instinctively that there is sweet meat inside; he just doesn't know how to get to it.

That, of course, has been my problem here. I had so many good stories and such a limited opportunity to pass some of my favorites along. And I sure always wanted to. So, even with my newfound social awareness and sensitivity, I really felt that I had to capture a few. If only for historical purposes.

You don't believe that? I guess acorns really don't fall too far from the tree.

Even grandfathers can't be good ALL the time.

ON PARTING THOUGHTS

Over a lifetime, things happen which remain permanently imprinted in the mind. They are not always what others might consider important. Why some of mine - innocuous to many, perhaps - remain so vivid after all these years is still inexplicable to me. They do not include weddings, childbirths, promotions or the many other delightful occasions that have brightened my life. But if you would like to walk back with me in time - in my shoes, with my thoughts, at those brief moments that I will try to recall for you - maybe you can see them, too.

KRISTEN

My oldest grand daughter already had an unusual start in life, having crossed the stage in her mother's womb as Sharon received her medical degree. She is now an absolutely lovely and talented young lady as she approaches her teens and we have a very close relationship. Not so when she was about six months old. As soon as she could stand up in her play pen, Kristen would maneuver herself so she could face me, wherever I might be sitting, and proceed to cuss me out to high heaven in baby gibberish only she apparently could understand. She would have a very serious frown on her face and if I said anything to her, she would get louder and louder. And she only did that to me. Why she wanted to bawl me out every time she saw me, I will never know. By the time she finally got old enough to talk, she had stopped doing it. I guess I must have straightened up by then.

ELIZABETH

It was a beautiful spring day. Elizabeth and I had joined Dave and Betty Boone, the Vice Chairman of CommerceAmerica Banking Company and his wife, for an outing at Churchill Downs. Elizabeth was just recovering from a near-death illness that had wasted her appearance from its early forties' still youthful fitness to that of a very elderly woman whose body and face were constantly drawn and wretched with pain. As we sat at a table outside the Kentucky Derby Museum, Dave and Betty excused themselves to visit the flower gardens while Elizabeth chose to rest. But she was happy and alive; and, in that moment, her blue eyes dancing and the golden highlights of her hair sparkling in the soft rays of the mid-day sun, smiling with the carefree promise of spring's - and her own - renewal, she was nineteen again. It was an image in time, moving back through a second chance at life. After all she had been through - after all we had been through - it was a beautiful spring day.

RUNAWAY

Elizabeth and I were at the Holiday Inn ocean front hotel in Jacksonville, Florida enjoying a late autumn vacation. The weather was chilly and overcast which kept us inside most of the day. Late in the morning, however, we had noticed a young girl, apparently in her mid-teens, who had come to the edge of the ocean drive and was sitting there staring out at the whitecaps that were whipping the cold water against the wide beach in front of our high-rise balcony. She did not seem to move for hours and, as the dinner hour approached, we became worried about her. After dressing to go out, I checked to see if she was still there and she was. We knew she probably hadn't eaten all day and neither Elizabeth nor I could go to dinner without my going down to see if she needed help. When I approached her, without knowing why except that our own daughter was near her age, I felt the same sadness I saw in her young, acne-marred face. When I inquired if anything was wrong, she looked up at me and said: "Honest, mister, I'm alright." After a brief, mostly one-sided conversation, I gave her enough money to get something to eat and to call home. She wouldn't take the money unless I agreed to accept, in return, the last soiled copy of "Watch Tower," a religious publication, she removed from an equally soiled and otherwise empty cloth bag. I took it and she walked away clutching the money in her hand. But she had promised, rather unconvincingly, that she would call home. I can't count the times I've prayed that she did.

WEATHER OR NOT

Our bank closed on Wednesday afternoon to compensate employees for Saturday morning hours. I usually used part of that time to catch up on things; but, this particular Wednesday I had promised Elizabeth that I would be home promptly at 1:00 P.M. to take her to play golf at Twilight Golf Course. Shortly after our noon closing time, it started raining cats and dogs so I continued with my work another hour or so. When I got home, I learned that downtown must have been hit with one of those "local" storms that never made it to our house. Elizabeth, and the golf course, had stayed completely dry. On the other hand, I got rained on twice that Wednesday afternoon.

CHARLIE

He was in the first or second grade. Hot weather had arrived early and I was going somewhere as school let out when I saw Charlie walking up the hill toward home. His closely cropped burr haircut contrasted sharply with the heavy winter coat he was wearing and he looked miserable in the heat. For some reason I may never fully understand, his condition caused more than a small tug at my heartstrings. I turned my car around, picked him up, took him home to get his little sister, and we went immediately to Bacon's Department Store to buy them both new spring jackets. I don't know why unwrapping Charlie, with his summer haircut, from his heavy winter coat was such a big deal. He could have taken off his coat and carried it. That would have relieved the misery in his face. But then I wouldn't have seen it. I was still fairly new at being a father. Maybe it was time I needed to take a deeper look at my growing responsibilities. Maybe it was really something else I was meant to see that day.

PERSONAL LIMITATIONS

Elizabeth had gone with Charlie, along with other den mothers and their little scouts, on an overnight camping trip. Sharon, then only five or six, stayed home with me. My project that Saturday was to repair a freshly broken pipe to the kitchen sink. I successfully removed the broken section and Sharon and I went to the hardware store to get a replacement. I installed the new section and, in the process, broke the section underneath it. Throughout the day, in continuing succession, I went to the hardware store, installed a new section of pipe, broke another piece, went back to the hardware store again until it was time for all sensible vendors of plumbing supplies to close for the weekend. Sharon, like me, had become very tired. In a last ditch effort to welcome Elizabeth and Charlie back home to a fully functional kitchen, I gathered all of the original pieces of broken pipe and headed off, with Sharon still in tow, to find a plumbing or hardware store still open. Everything was closed in Jeffersonville and Clarksville but I got to one in New Albany just as they were locking up. They must have seen my brand of frustration before - an armful of broken pipes and a very tired little girl who had long since lost the thrill of visiting hardware stores - so they let me in. Someone took my broken pipes, grease trap and couplings to some secret place and assembled a metal miracle for me. They even cut off parts of the standard length pipes that didn't fit my layout - a little problem I may have overlooked before. I took the whole assembly home, followed the good man's instructions with respect to putty and sealants, tightened a few clamps and turned on the water. It worked! Sharon and I both slept like babies that night. I woke up Sunday morning with a better understanding of my personal limitations. Plumbing had just made it to the top of the list.

SHARON

She was undergoing a routine tonsillectomy but when your little girl, only two or three years old, is in the operating room for any reason, the waiting is interminable. Then, when the post operative care requires more than the standard recovery period, young parents can become very anxious. The staff assured us that everything was fine but we were not allowed to go into the recovery room. They did, however, let us see her through the window of the door. She was still unconscious lying on the gurney, as pale as a ghost, with her light blond hair adding to the lifeless vision. The blood that had trickled down her tiny cheeks and chin was clearly and painfully visible. Sharon eventually came out from under the anesthesia and she recovered fine. I don't think I ever will.

LEGENDS

I have met a few famous people over the years - Mohammed Ali, Tom T. Hall, Donald Trump, Burt Bacharach - and have seen or been in the company of many others. One stands alone. When I was in the Army, stationed in Fontainebleau, France, our small company was put aboard a bus and taken to a theater in Paris. Bob Hope was in town and had decided to do something special - apparently spontaneous and unplanned - for all the American servicemen stationed in the area. We knew that he had entertained American troops during World War II; however, this happened during the mid 1950's, in France, during peacetime and far removed from any dread of combat. But we were over there serving our country, a long way from home, and Bob Hope wanted us to be entertained for an evening, too. We heard that he had rented the theater; recruited singers, dancers and musicians from the Paris entertainment scene; and, personally had obtained permission from the military command to put on that fabulous show for us. No one, it seems, had asked him to do what he did; but he made a bunch of young soldiers very happy that night. That was Bob Hope up there on the stage - becoming a legend to us already - long before he became one to the world.

ESCARGOT

My friend, Tommy, and I were in Paris one afternoon when he decided he wanted something special to eat. We stopped at one of the nicer sidewalk cafes and he ordered escargot and a glass of wine. Since I never ate anything I couldn't spell, I just had wine. As he explained the delicate flavor of the fine food he had ordered - prepared in a butter, garlic and wine sauce - I thought I may have made a mistake by not ordering some too. But when they brought his plate, I couldn't believe my eyes. They were snails! Those same slimy little creatures that crawled all over our woodpiles back home! Tommy used a small silver pick to extract every delectable morsel out of those all too familiar little shells as I sat there in partial disbelief and partial disgust. Tommy was from Indianapolis. You would have thought they had woodpiles up there, too.

EMERGING HISTORY

During my brief stay in San Bernardino, California in 1951 and 1952, my junior year in high school, a favorite eating place when I had the money was a unique type of fast food restaurant, with golden arches, called McDonald's. You could buy a hamburger and French fries for a quarter and for another twenty cents you could get a milkshake. And you could get it quick. As tight as money was then, I really appreciated their fine, cheap service. I did not know until many years later that this was the original (and only) restaurant of the McDonald brothers. Theirs was the concept Ray Kroc would soon acquire and turn into the worldwide icon it has become today.

... AND FINALLY

As a young boy, I had many scrapes with death. You don't live among rattlesnakes and copperheads, dive off of high rocks into shallow water, or jump from a mill roof on to sawdust piles embedded with sharp scraps of wood without cheating the grim reaper ever once in a while. But the one childhood experience that remains most vivid came when my cousins, little brother and I were playing Tarzan. We had found a tall tree with a grapevine that looked strong enough to use to swing across a deep ravine to the other side. I was the older of the four boys playing together and I used that status to be the first to try it out. Midway across, the grapevine broke and I found myself sitting upright at the bottom of the ravine on the only mossy spot of clear ground that could have saved me from total disaster. I was completely surrounded by large, treacherous rocks - literally within inches of me in all directions - and a collapse of my body at the end of the fall, especially backward, could well have been fatal. That one small mossy piece of earth and that miraculous landing convinced me, later on, that someone, or something, spotted a fragile grapevine and threw out a lifeline to a careless little boy that day.

As I edge ever closer to its natural and more ordinary end, I only hope I have made it a life worth saving.

ADDENDUM

SELECTED ILLUSTRATIONS

The following section contains selected copies of the pen-and ink illustrations from which the color images within the text of these perspectives were derived. Although they represent a work-for-hire, the artist's work is greatly appreciated for the manner in which she was able to capture the essence of the characters or situations being depicted.

Unfortunately, constraints within the publication process does not permit the inclusion of all the illustration nor does it allow the reader to fully experience the quality of presentation of the originals. They truly are beautiful works of art.

Regardless, please enjoy these examples of the work of the talented Georgia Lee Farr in as close to their original state as our limited abilities could reproduce them.

THE GARAGE SALE

THE SCRAMBLE TO SAVE OUR HIDES

THE RESTFUL WAY OF A MOUNTAIN MAN

WAITING FOR MOMMAW

THE GYPSY CAVES OF GRANADA

BETTER TO BRING HIM HOME THAN BEAT HIM UP

103

ELVIS AND ME

"I LIKE TO WIN!"

EDUCATION IN A ONE-ROOM SCHOOL

A SCARED WALK THROUGH THE WOODS

A SOBERING MOMENT

THAT RISKY "LOOK OF LOVE"

109

GOING TO GET ANOTHER BEER

GOOD BYE---

THANKS FOR
TAKING THE TIME
TO VISIT.

GENE HENSLEY